Lovestories 4 Girls

Last Chance for a First Date

Priyanka Banerji

Compact Verlag

Bisher sind in dieser Reihe erschienen:

Band 1: Full Moon Kisses
Band 2: Last Chance for a First Date
Band 3: Flirt But Don't Fall in Love
Band 4: Trouble in Seventh Heaven

Weitere Titel sind in Vorbereitung.

Chefredaktion: Dr. Angela Sendlinger
Redaktion: Paulina Palomino
Fachredaktion: Monika Bowler
Produktion: Wolfram Friedrich
Illustrationen: Bettina Weisl (MA Illustration)
Typografischer Entwurf: textum GmbH
Umschlaggestaltung: Bettina Weisl (MA Illustration)

ISBN: 978-3-8174-7825-5
7278251

Besuche uns im Internet: www.compactverlag.de

Vorwort

Mit dieser spannenden und romantischen Compact Lovestory kannst du deine Englischkenntnisse spielend leicht verbessern. Eine deutsche Einleitung vor jedem neuen Kapitel hilft dir, den englischen Text zu verstehen. Außerdem werden auf jeder Seite die etwas schwierigeren Wörter erklärt, und durch die Zeichnungen bekommst du eine genauere Vorstellung von den vier Girls und ihren aufregenden Erlebnissen. Blätter doch einfach mal durch!

Jedes Kapitel wird durch Übungen und Tests ergänzt, die richtig spannend und abwechslungsreich sind: Da geht es um Jungs und Liebe, Partys, Freundschaft und Mode – so wird Englisch lernen richtig spannend und cool!

Die Antworten und Lösungen kannst du gleich ins Buch schreiben und hinterher im Lösungsteil nachlesen, ob du alles richtig gemacht hast und was die Tests über dich aussagen. Und wenn du möchtest, kannst du alle Vokabeln im Glossar noch einmal nachschlagen. Slang-Ausdrücke sind mit einem ϟ gekennzeichnet.

Wir wünschen dir viel Spaß mit Evie und ihren Freundinnen – und natürlich viel Erfolg beim Englisch lernen!

Inhalt

Kapitel 1: The Meeting 5

Kapitel 2: Party Night 27

Kapitel 3: Back to School 49

Kapitel 4: Misunderstandings 69

Kapitel 5: Last Chance for a First Date 91

Lösungen 112

Glossar 119

1

The Meeting

1

Heute Morgen hat Evie es besonders eilig. Sie muss unbedingt den Schulbus erwischen, mit dem Nick fährt, ihr neuer Schwarm. Leider gelingt es ihr auch dieses Mal nicht, ihn anzusprechen. Evie muss sich etwas anderes einfallen lassen: Während der Mathestunde hat sie plötzlich eine geniale Idee. Sie will eine Geburtstagsparty für ihre Freundin Emily organisieren und alle Schüler ihres Jahrgangs einladen – auch Nick! Mit diesem Plan muss es einfach klappen, bestimmt werden sie und Nick auf der Party zusammenkommen …

"Olly, get a move on! We need to go, we're already ten minutes late and Miss Hamilton will be angry if my geography homework is late again!"
A dishevelled Olly ran out of the bathroom, complete with wet hair and a towel around his waist.
"What! You've only just come out of the shower? What have you been doing for the last hour?!"
Olly simply looked amazed at his sister who stood by the front door, fully dressed and ready to go. And was that eyeliner and purple eye shadow he could see? What was happening? She had never been ready on time before, or

had ever worn make-up to school and it was only half-past seven!
Before he even had a chance to respond, his sister slammed the front door and left without saying goodbye.

⚡ Get a move on!	Los, mach schon!
dishevelled	unordentlich
waist	Taille
amazed	verwundert
to slam	zuschlagen
bothered	beunruhigt
crush	Schwarm
broad-shouldered	breitschultrig
to blush	erröten
to startle from	aufschrecken aus
embarrassing	peinlich
bumpy	holperig

Evie wasn't really bothered by what Miss Hamilton would say. She was more interested in the fact that she would miss her bus. Whatever she did, she could not miss the seven forty-five bus! Evie usually walked to school in the morning, but today, she knew her latest crush was on that bus and she did not want to miss yet another opportunity to say hello to him.

Nicholas Montgomery, or Nick, was a dark-haired, broad-shouldered football player on the school's mixed football team who made Evie blush when she heard his name. The bus driver startled Evie from her embarrassing thoughts, so she quickly bought her ticket and sat down with the other students from her school.
As the bus started on the bumpy road, she turned her head to see if she could see Nick. She was just about to give up

the idea that he might be on the bus, when at last she noticed him at the back.

Nick was listening to his MP3 player while looking out of the window. He was wearing the tie loosely around his neck in a cool manner. He kept the top three buttons of his shirt open and he had thrown his school bag casually across his shoulder. Nick's hair was dark, barely touching his eyebrows, and... Evie stopped. She could not bring herself to look into his dark-green eyes, because she would immediately shudder if they made eye contact.

Übung 1: What's up with Evie? Kreuze die richtigen Aussagen an!

Evie is...

- [x] ready to go.
- [ ] late.
- [x] painted.
- [x] leaving without saying goodbye.
- [ ] very nice to her older brother.
- [x] in love with someone.
- [ ] not interested in boys at all.

Evie had never really had a big crush on someone before, but this time she instinctively knew that this could become something more than just a crush.

She had met him for the first time outside school hours on the football field. He was coming out of the boys' changing rooms, while she was walking out of the girls'.

casually	lässig
barely	kaum, fast
to shudder	zittern
to have a crush on sb.	in jmd. verknallt sein
changing room	Umkleidekabine

shy	schüchtern
to bend down	niederknien
lace	Schnürsenkel
to come undone	aufgehen
to glance	blicken
to shrug one's shoulders	mit den Schultern zucken
jog off	loslaufen
to join sb.	zu jmd. hingehen

They had been looking at one another, but neither had spoken a word. However, during football practice that day, Nick kept looking in her direction and she kept looking at him.

Over the weeks, they were too shy to speak to each other, although they were both known to be talking a lot at school.

Then one day, Nick had bent down to tie his football boot laces that had come undone during the match. He looked up, saw Evie standing right beside him and had said "Hi!". That was the first time he had spoken to her. But instead of responding, Evie had blushed and glanced back down at him, saying nothing in return. Nick had looked disappointed, and had shrugged his shoulders. Then he had jogged off to join the rest of his team. Ever since that day, Evie promised herself that the next time she saw him, she would speak to him first.

Suddenly, Evie was once again startled from her daydream: Nick was making his way down the bus, directly to where she was sitting. She couldn't believe it – he was going to speak to her again! This time however, things would be different, because she was prepared to talk to him. Today, she wasn't wearing her sweaty football shirt, but instead she had put on purple eye shadow, some eyeliner and had applied some new perfume just before she had left the house.

But just as she was about to whisper, "Ah, Nick, you shouldn't have!" Nick walked straight past her and stepped off the bus.

Evie hadn't noticed that the bus had stopped outside the school grounds. She thought the situation was incredibly embarrassing, especially because one of her classmates – Toby – had noticed and winked at her on the way out. She just wished that round-faced Toby would find his own girlfriend and leave her alone!

sweaty	verschwitzt
to apply	auftragen, auflegen
to whisper	flüstern
to step off	aussteigen
incredibly	unglaublich
to wink at sb.	jmd. zuzwinkern
round-faced	pausbackig
belongings	Siebensachen
grateful	dankbar
to chat	quatschen

Evie took all her belongings in a hurry, left the bus and breathed in the fresh, cool morning air. When she looked around, she was grateful to see her friend Nina in the distance. She called out to Nina and soon the two girls started chatting and laughing and they slowly walked to the school building together. This made Evie forget about her embarrassing situation during the bus journey.

Übung 2: Choose the right word!
Vervollständige die Sätze mit den passenden Wörtern!

~~casually~~ ~~startled~~ ~~crush~~ ~~turned~~

~~incredibly~~ ~~glanced~~

1. Evie ....turned....... her head to see if she could see Nick.
2. They ....glanced.... at one another.
3. Evie was once again ....startled..... from her daydream.
4. Nick had thrown his school bag ....casually.... across his shoulder.
5. Evie had never really had a big ....crush.... on someone before.
6. Evie thought the situation was ....incredibly.... embarrassing.

In the afternoon, the four girls – Holly, Emily, Nina and Evie – went to their final class of the day. Maths was Evie's least favourite subject; she tried to avoid solving algebraic expressions wherever possible. Instead, she tried to think of something more interesting. It was Emily's birthday soon and they had to arrange something for her. What could the girls do? Maybe they could all plan a surprise birthday party!

Their teacher, Mrs Skelton, had set them all difficult exercises and separated the whole class into groups of three. As a result, a quiet murmur had broken out in the classroom. Evie, Nina and Holly were in a group together, but Emily was with two other girls. So Evie took this as a great opportunity to tell her two friends about her ideas for Emily's party.

to avoid	vermeiden
algebraic expression	algebraische Gleichung
to set exercises	Übungen aufgeben
murmur	Murmeln
ϟ Guys!	Leute!
sort sth. out	etw. klären, planen
invitation	Einladung
to overhear	hören
fussy	wählerisch, aufgeregt

"Guys! I think we should sort out Emily's party. It's next week and we need to send out invitations soon if we're going to have a party!"

Evie kept her voice down to avoid Emily overhearing their conversation.

"Yeah, definitely," Nina agreed, "but what should we do? She's quite fussy about her birthday plans this year, because it's her fifteenth!"

to mention	erwähnen
to exclaim	rufen, ausrufen
fancy-dress party	Mottoparty
to nod (in agreement)	(zustimmend) nicken
⚡ funky	abgefahren
to dress up	sich verkleiden, sich schick machen
eventually	schließlich, letztendlich
to convince	überzeugen

"I know, but I think we could have a party at my house. My parents are away on holiday next weekend, and two of my brothers are going to watch a rugby match. They are staying over at a friend's place, so we could have the house to ourselves that weekend!"

However, what Evie didn't mention to her two friends was that she also had plans to invite Nick to this party. Evie had not told any of her friends about him. Although she did not like to keep any secrets from her friends, she just couldn't tell them about her crush on Nick.

"That's a great idea!" Holly exclaimed. "I think we should think about ideas for a fancy-dress party though. We've had a lot of house parties this year and they've all been pretty much the same. Maybe we could have a *Bollywood* party?"

Nina nodded in agreement. "That's a really good idea. But because there's not a lot of time to sort things out, we could have a 60s party instead? We could make funky invitations and invite the whole year."

Evie had to admit that she did like the idea of Holly's *Bollywood* party. She had already started to think about what Nick would look like dressed up as an Indian actor.

Between them, Holly and Evie decided upon the *Bollywood* party and eventually convinced Nina, too, that it was a good idea. They made plans to write the invitations and send them out by Friday. Since it was only Tuesday, they just had a few days to sort everything out.

Übung 3: Unscramble the words! Ordne die Buchstaben zu sinnvollen Wörtern.

1. ittavinion — i nvitation
2. tapyr — p arty
3. prissure — s ureprise
4. dibrathy — b irthday
5. fittou — o utfit
6. loodyBlow — B ollywood
7. eida — i dea
8. tersce — s ecret

hip	Hüfte
furious	wütend

The girls were so excited about the party planning, they forgot all about their maths class! Mrs Skelton was now standing over the girls with her hands on her hips – she looked furious!

"Girls! I do hope that when I hear about *Bollywood* from the other side of the classroom that it is somehow related to mathematics?! I see your friend Emily here has the right idea. In fact...", she turned around to face the entire classroom now, "in fact, I do believe Emily is the only one here with any idea of how to pass the upcoming mock maths exam! Now I don't want any of you to be discussing boys, *Bollywood*, or anything similar; I want the exercises to be solved in silence!"

entire	ganz, gesamt
upcoming	anstehend
mock exam	Probeprüfung
amazingly	überraschend, erstaunlich
surprise	Überraschung
to realize	feststellen, bemerken
ecstatic	total begeistert

And with that, the entire classroom fell silent.

Over the next few days, the girls started to create the invitations. Holly was the most creative and so she began to design authentic Indian invitations.

She was amazingly quick and, by Friday, the invitations were done.

To keep the party a surprise for Emily, Holly had written "Emily's surprise birthday party" on the invitations, but the whole year seemed to be discussing it. Emily eventually realized what was happening and was ecstatic to find out that her best friends were planning a party for her fifteenth birthday!

hug	Umarmung
weakly	schwach
to reassure sb.	jmd. beruhigen
relieved	erleichtert
to be positive	ganz sicher sein
to recognize	(an)erkennen
≠ invite	Einladung

"Oh Evie, you're the best!" she said, giving her a big hug on Friday afternoon.

Evie smiled weakly. She felt sad and disappointed that the birthday party was no longer a surprise for Emily.

When she noticed Evie's disappointment, Emily tried to reassure her, "Evie! The whole year was invited, so it would have been impossible to leave it a surprise birthday party as well! But Evie, I'm just so happy that the party is going to be on my birthday! You know that I just love Indian food!"

"Oh, Emily, are you sure?" Evie asked, very relieved.

"I'm positive, Eve", Emily smiled, "but can we now just discuss the party arrangements and what to wear?! I'm so excited about the *Bollywood* party theme! We need to wear extra special outfits now!"

The entire school seemed to know about the fancy-dress party. In the days before Emily's birthday, people who Evie didn't even recognize started thanking her for the party invite. She asked Holly how many invitations she had sent, because everyone now wanted to come to the girls' *Bollywood* party!

The only person who didn't know about the arrangements for the party was Evie's older brother, Olly. He was planning to have the house to himself that weekend and he first

annoyed	verärgert
neither ..., nor	weder ..., noch

came to know about the *Bollywood* party from an invitation Holly had given him. Ever since that morning on which Evie had left home without saying goodbye, the two of them were not really speaking to each other. Therefore Evie had forgotten to inform him about the party.

Olly was annoyed because he had planned to invite a few guys around to watch the rugby match on TV. Instead, he would now have to "babysit" his sister's party next weekend. He would have to make sure their house was not completely ruined before their parents returned from holiday. Olly didn't really like the party theme either. The party invitation mentioned that everybody had to dress up and he was neither a fan of fancy-dress, nor a fan of *Bollywood*.

Übung 4: Match-up. Finde das passende Gegenteil!

1.	before	answer
2.	ask	after
3.	older	pleased
4.	without	a lot
5.	annoyed	younger
6.	a few	with

to confront sb.	jmd. zur Rede stellen
to burst into laughter	in Gelächter ausbrechen
something she could not argue with	etwas, wogegen sie nichts sagen konnte
insistent	hartnäckig
to be honest	um ehrlich zu sein
worth the effort	die Mühe wert
what's more	darüber hinaus, außerdem
to upset	verärgern

Two days before the actual party, he confronted Evie in the corridor and tested her to see how important he was to the party arrangements. He simply said, "Evie, you can't have this party. I just won't allow it."

Evie looked surprised and was waiting for him to burst into laughter to tell her that he was joking, but he looked incredibly serious. Olly had never had a problem with her party arrangements before. In fact, Olly had always helped her out.

Evie responded in a casual tone, "Olly, I know you're joking, so just stop it."

But this time, Olly looked at Evie with his most serious face and said, "I'll tell Mum and Dad."

This was something Evie knew she could not argue with, because she had planned to at least keep the party a secret from her parents.

"Look Olly, I don't know what's happened to you recently. What's wrong? Why are you suddenly being so annoying?"

But Olly was insistent this time. "Eve, you didn't even bother to let me know that I need to sort out an Indian outfit by Saturday, plus take care of absolutely everyone you've invited. So, to be honest, Eve, I don't know if it's even worth the effort! I only found out about the party from a pretty little invitation card from Holly. The fact is, you didn't even tell me about it! What's more, you've recently been wearing all this make-up to school and you leave for school before me. We always used to travel to school together and you always used to wait for me! So, what's going on, Eve?!"

This time, Olly knew he had won. Evie blushed at the mention of make-up, looked down at her shoes and seemed really sorry for upsetting her brother. Olly knew he didn't need to know anything else and surprised Evie with the biggest grin across his face.

"You silly monkey, you knew I was joking, why did you take me so seriously?!"

Übung 5: Say it in German! Übersetze die folgenden Begriffe.

1. secret ....
2. recently ....
3. suddenly ....
4. insistent ....
5. to blush ....
6. a big grin ....

Evie looked half angry, but half relieved to see that her brother was still the same old Olly. She playfully hit him on the arm, but then gave him a quick kiss on the cheek.

playfully	spielerisch
siblings	Geschwister
embarrass-ment	Verlegenheit
to borrow	ausleihen

At the end of the school day, the two siblings walked back home together. When they were turning around their street corner, Olly questioned Evie again, "But seriously, Eve, what is it with all the make-up?!"
To hide her embarrassment, Evie walked even faster and tried not to look at the grin across Olly's face.
He smiled and simply said, "I think you should wear your new eye shadow for the party on Saturday; that colour really suits you."
Evie simply blushed and looked away, because this time, she knew Olly wasn't being sarcastic.

The night before the party, Holly and Nina came over to help Olly and Evie set up the house for the party. Holly had bought the decorations and Nina had baked a cake for Emily. This time, they had all been very careful not to tell Emily any of the details. Although the party was no longer a secret, they had one more surprise for her at the party itself! The girls were busy putting up "Happy Birthday" banners around the house. Holly started placing the decorations she had bought from a local Indian store around the whole house.

Meanwhile, Evie was busy in the kitchen. She was preparing a delicious spicy Indian curry – she had borrowed the recipe from her Indian friend Anita. Olly had been to an Indian supermarket to buy some snacks. He had also bought a lot of bottles of soft drinks and he had even tried to make a special Indian drink called lassi!

By the time they had finished decorating the house, it was almost midnight. Everything looked really splendid and most authentic for the *Bollywood* party. Both Nina and Holly had brought over their sleeping bags to stay the night. So the exhausted girls now lay their sleeping bags in the living room downstairs. There they started to talk about the boys who were coming to the party. At this point, Olly felt it was best to leave the room. He went into the kitchen to make some hot chocolate instead.

splendid	fantastisch
sleeping bag	Schlafsack
exhausted	erschöpft
remarkably	bemerkens-wert
ϟ fit	attraktiv
good-looking	gut aussehend
close	eng befreundet, nah

Nina started talking first. "Girls, there is this remarkably fit guy from our year... Nick! Have you seen him around? He's really good friends with a few people I know and he's in a couple of my lessons!"

To Evie's surprise, Nina knew Nick from class, and thought he was pretty good-looking.

Holly agreed, "Yeah, he is good-looking but, to be honest, I've seen him flirting with the prettiest girls from our year. I also saw him standing outside school recently with an attractive blonde girl! I don't know who she is, but they seemed pretty close..."

Übung 6: Do you have a "crush"? Teste, ob du wirklich verliebt bist.

1. How often do you think of him?
   a) ❑ When you are supposed to do a school project together.
   b) ❑ Once or twice a week.
   c) ❑ Every moment.

2. When he walks past you, what do you feel?
   a) ❑ Nothing.
   b) ❑ Lots of butterflies in my stomach.
   c) ❑ My heart feels weak.

3. How long have you felt attracted to him?
   a) ❑ I'm not attracted to him.
   b) ❑ Just recently – it felt right one day.
   c) ❑ A long time – more than a few months.

4. When he talks to another girl, what do you feel?
   a) ❑ He is free to talk to anyone, why should I care?
   b) ❑ Uncomfortable, I don't like it. I feel jealous.
   c) ❑ I feel pain in my heart.

mug	Becher, große Tasse
to be able to do sth.	etw. tun können
disappointment	Enttäuschung

It was probably very good timing that Olly came in just then with four mugs of steaming hot chocolate, so Evie was able to hide her disappointment.

2

Party Night

2

Evie, Holly, Nina und Olly haben alles für die Bollywood-Party vorbereitet. Nun können sie es kaum erwarten, dass die Gäste eintreffen. Als endlich alle fröhlich feiern, steht Evie etwas verloren herum und hält Ausschau nach Nick. Wo bleibt der bloß? Schließlich kommt er – mit einem auffallend hübschen Mädchen an seiner Seite! Evie ist total enttäuscht und gesteht ihren Freundinnen, dass sie in Nick verknallt ist. Da ist natürlich erstmal Kriegsrat angesagt: Gemeinsam beraten die Freundinnen, was Evie jetzt tun soll …

Finally, it was the night of the party, but no-one had arrived yet. The three girls were patiently waiting at Evie's house for their guests to arrive. They had told Emily a different starting time for the party, so that the girls could surprise her. But why hadn't the rest of the invited guests arrived? The party invitations had clearly stated 7 p.m. and it was already nearly a quarter to eight!

In the living room, where the girls were waiting, Evie was surprisingly quiet. She was still thinking about what Holly had said the night before. What if Nick already had a girl-friend? Now that no-one was going to arrive at her party, she felt upset and very disappointed. The girls had started to get ready at six and at that time, she was happy to dress up in her Indian outfit.

Evie was wearing a long purple skirt decorated with pearls around the border and a small Indian blouse which showed her slim curves. She also wore a long Indian scarf around her shoulders and a purple bindi in the middle of her forehead. Some shiny purple jewellery and a beautiful necklace that Olly had bought for her at an Indian store completed her exotic look. She looked really beautiful!

Holly and Nina were also wearing their traditional Indian outfits. Nina had borrowed a blouse from an Indian friend: its turquoise blue colour looked lovely against her blue eyes. Holly wore a long pink top, a necklace and white trousers. She had also wrapped a shawl that she had borrowed from Evie around her shoulders. But Olly was still getting ready upstairs. He did not seem too bothered by the guests' late arrival, because he still hadn't even decided upon his outfit...

patiently	geduldig
clearly	deutlich
to state	angeben, festsetzen
pearl	Perle
border	Saum
scarf	Halstuch
bindi	Bindi, (Schmuck-) Punkt auf der Stirn
forehead	Stirn
shiny	funkelnd, glänzend
necklace	Halskette
to wrap	einschlagen, (um)wickeln
shawl	Schal

Just as Evie was giving up all hope that people were going to arrive at their party at all, Holly exclaimed: “Look girls, there they are!”

***Übung 7:** Adjectives and Adverbs. Bilde jeweils aus dem Adjektiv ein Adverb!*

1. quick ....
2. clear ....
3. near ....
4. surprised ....
5. beautiful ....
6. patient ....
7. final ....
8. exotic ....
9. happy ....

The three girls quickly looked out of Evie's living room window and saw a large group of young people in beautiful Indian costumes walking down the street.

Evie had to admit that all their friends looked very beautiful. Not to anyone's surprise, the boys looked more casually dressed. Most boys wore jeans, shirts and one or two of them even wore a waistcoat.

Evie wasted no time and ran to the front door to greet her guests. But as she opened it, the first guest to arrive was Emily! She could barely recognize her best friend. Emily had her hair tied back and she wore a beautiful long top with a white silk scarf. She had applied her make-up really well and her outfit looked fantastic.

waistcoat	Weste
to waste time	Zeit verschwenden
silk	Seide

"WOW! Emily, look at you, you look amazing!" "Thanks, Eve, but you look fantastic in your outfit, too!", Emily said and moved slowly away from the crowded entrance.

"Thanks, Em! But I was really scared for a while, because I didn't know why everyone had come so late..." Evie said this in a low whisper so that no-one could listen to their conversation. Nina and Holly now welcomed the other guests and Evie was able to speak to Emily.

"Oh Eve, I forgot to say! I didn't realize that you only told me to come at 8 p.m.! I thought you had made a mistake on the invitations, because you told me to arrive at eight o'clock and not at seven, so I made sure everybody in our year knew about the change in time!"

crowded	überfüllt
entrance	Eingang
to be scared	Angst haben
to hug	umarmen
to cheer	jubeln, klatschen
to seem	erscheinen
uneasy	unbehaglich
to spot	sehen, entdecken

Evie laughed and hugged her friend. "Ha-ha, you are silly, Emily! But anyway, I almost forgot to say... Happy Birthday!"

Evie said this much louder so that all the guests could hear her. Everybody in the whole house began to cheer and sing "Happy Birthday" to Emily. Emily was extremely happy. She couldn't believe the party was really just for her.

Suddenly, Olly came into the room with the huge cake Nina had baked for Emily. But what was Olly wearing?

He had finally dressed up for the party, wearing a white shirt with jeans. However, he had also pinned a white shawl onto his shirt and he was wearing a turban on his head! Everyone started to cheer for Olly, especially Emily, who found his outfit quite amusing.

After Olly's arrival with the cake, everybody sat down to enjoy the party. Everything looked really good and everyone seemed extremely happy. People were laughing, some of the guests started eating and a few even tried out Indian dancing in the living room. Emily and Olly were talking on the sofa and Nina joined her boyfriend, Marcus.

Evie was standing alone in the living room, looking at her guests. Everyone seemed to be enjoying the party. But Evie was not as happy as she could have been. She felt uneasy. She was missing someone... She looked around for Nick and after a few minutes realized that he hadn't arrived yet.

"Eve, it looks great, doesn't it?"

Holly, who noticed that Evie was standing alone at her own party, came over to speak to her.

"Yeah, it does."

"Are you okay though? Why are you standing around here on your own? What's wrong?"

"Well, nothing, just the usual..."

Evie stopped suddenly, she had just spotted him. She had left the front door open, because many people were arriving late to the party. One of them to arrive late

Hang on a second!	Warte eine Sekunde!

was Nick. Now he was coming through the front door, but he wasn't alone!

"Look Evie, there's that boy I was talking about last night. That's Nick, over there!", Holly said to Evie, who looked as though she had just seen a ghost.

"And see, just like I said, Eve, he's with a new girl every time I see him. But oh, hang on a second, I think that's the same girl I saw him talking to outside school. Pretty, isn't she?"

However, Evie wasn't listening. She was staring at the girl and thinking how happy Nick looked with her. The girl had long blonde hair and green eyes, just like his. She was wearing a beautiful Indian dress with a beautiful pink scarf. Evie thought that the girl almost looked like an Indian princess and she immediately felt a little jealous.

Evie really liked Nick, but sometimes she found it strange that she liked him so much. She didn't even know him that well, but every time she saw him, she had butterflies in her stomach. She felt embarrassed and turned away. She was not even aware that Holly tapped her on the shoulder.

jealous	eifersüchtig
to have butterflies in one's stomach	Schmetterlinge im Bauch haben
to turn away	sich abwenden
to be aware	merken, sich bewusst sein
to tap on sb.'s shoulder	jmd. auf die Schulter klopfen
to manage to do sth.	schaffen, etw. zu tun

"Eve... Evie, what's wrong? You look like you've just seen a ghost, you've turned quite pale! Are you okay?"
"I'm... fine", Evie managed to say to make sure that her friend didn't worry.
"No, you are not fine at all! Eve, come on, I'm your friend. You have to tell me what's wrong!"

Übung 8: True or false? Kreuze an!

1. The boys were...
   - ❑ more casually dressed.
   - ❑ more casual dressed.

2. Everyone seemed to be...
   - ❑ enjoying the party.
   - ❑ joining the party.

3. "I don't know why...
   - ❑ everyone went so late."
   - ❑ everyone came so late."

4. The girl was wearing a beautiful...
   - ❑ Indish dress.
   - ❑ Indian dress.

5. Everybody in the whole house...
   - ❑ begun to cheer and sing.
   - ❑ began to cheer and sing.

6. Suddenly Evie felt...
   - ❑ a little jealous.
   - ❑ a little jealousy.

7. Evie found it strange...
   - ❑ that Nick liked her so much.
   - ❑ that she liked Nick so much.

8. Every time she saw him...
   - ❑ she heard butterflies in her stomach.
   - ❑ she had butterflies in her stomach.

By now, Nick had taken his 'blonde girl' to the kitchen to look for some food, so Evie felt more relaxed. She didn't know if it was a good idea to tell her friend about this or not. None of them knew about her crush on Nick, but then, she was going to have to tell them soon. She would have preferred to tell Emily first, who was her best friend. But it was Emily's day today and she looked so happy talking to Olly on the sofa. Evie thought it was best not to disturb them. So she decided to tell Holly the whole story.

none of them	keine von ihnen
to prefer	bevorzugen
actually	eigentlich
curious	neugierig

"Yeah, Holly, I do have something to say actually. Let's sit down and I will explain you..."

The girls sat down together on the floor. By now, Holly was extremely curious to find out what would follow. "Come on, what's up with you?" she started to question Evie.

Evie began, "I've been meaning to tell you guys for a while now, but I was just a bit embarrassed and so I hadn't told you before..."

Holly cried out and said, "Oh, Eve! Please tell me, is it about a boy?!"

This was why Evie had never really told the girls before. Holly, for example, was such a romantic and really loved talking about boys. But Evie enjoyed talking about sport and never really spoke about boys before, so this was something new for her.

to cry out	aufschreien, ausrufen
romantic	Romantikerin
to suppose	vermuten
to stand up	aufstehen

"Yeah, I suppose it is," she responded. Holly was ecstatic!

"Oh, good, go on, what's he like, what's his name?!"

"Holly, you know him already; he's the guy who has just come through the door...".

Before Evie had even finished the sentence, Holly said:

"Nick? You have a crush on Nick?! Eve, come on, he's always with different girls. You might know him better than me of course... he seems like a nice guy... but are you sure about this?"

This was a very strange reaction from Holly, who was always so positive about boys. She had never before spoken like this about any boy. Now Evie stood up and listened to her friend carefully.

Übung 9: How is Evie feeling? Ergänze die Sätze und finde heraus, wie Evie sich fühlt.

wants *guy* *friends* *blonde*

final *upset*

1. Is Nick really a nice .... ▢ .... ?
2. Before making any .... ▢ .... decisions, Evie wants to speak to her friends.
3. Holly .... ▢ to know what's wrong with Evie.
4. Evie was looking sad and ▢ .... by now.
5. Evie wants to tell her .... ▢ .... about her crush.
6. The girl at Nick's side has .... ▢ hair.

Evie feels ....

"But why do you say that, Holly? To be honest, I don't know him too well. I've just watched him play football a few times and he looks pretty good... Do you think I'm being foolish?"

"No, of course you're not, Eve. I just think you should be careful with boys like him... I'll tell you what, I'm going to go call Emily and Nina, so we can all decide what to do."

Evie was looking quite sad and upset by now, but she thought it was best to speak to her friends before making any final decisions. So the girls got up to leave. As they stood up, Nick and his 'blonde' friend came over and sat down exactly where they were sitting before! He saw Evie and smiled at her, but she looked down again. Now she just wasn't so sure anymore.

foolish	dumm
decision	Entscheidung
Was it just Evie?	Kam es Evie nur so vor?
ϟ to fancy sb.	jmd. toll finden
towards	nach, in Richtung

They found Emily and Olly sitting on the sofa eating birthday cake. Was it just Evie, or was Olly flirting a little with Emily? She thought it best not to mention anything about that in front of Holly, because she had a feeling that Holly had fancied Olly before. But Holly didn't seem too bothered and went over to the sofa with Evie.

"I think Evie wants to speak to you for a moment, Emily, if that's okay?" Holly looked directly towards Emily and ignored Olly completely.

Olly looked surprised and before he could say anything, Holly quickly took both Emily and Evie by the hand and led them away. Olly thought it best not to ask and went over to the kitchen to get some more birthday cake. Holly took both her friends to the place close to where Nina and Marcus were sitting. They were too busy holding hands and talking in soft whispers to notice the three girls coming directly towards them. So when Holly called out, "Nina!", Marcus was so surprised that he nearly fell off his seat.

"Sorry about that, Marcus!" Holly said, "We were just wondering if we could speak to Nina for a moment? Olly is in the kitchen, if you want to speak to him – I think he's gone to get some more cake!"

to lead sb. away	jmd. wegführen
to talk in whispers	im Flüsterton sprechen
to fall off	runterfallen
to wonder	sich fragen, überlegen
all of a sudden	plötzlich, mit einem Mal

Evie was feeling terrible disturbing the party like this. All of a sudden, she felt extremely uneasy and didn't want to tell anyone about her feelings. Marcus, who still looked quite surprised, gave Nina a quick kiss on the cheek and went to find Olly. The girls rushed upstairs into Evie's room, so that no-one could overhear their conversation. Holly started speaking first.

"Well, sorry to trouble you, girls, but we have a problem. I know it's Emily's birthday party tonight, but this is really important. Eve?"

to shriek out	hinausschreien

Evie looked at Holly, then across to Emily and Nina. She took a deep breath and said, "I fancy Nick Montgomery."

This time it was Nina who shrieked out, "Aaaaah, Evie! That's amazing! When? How? Why didn't you tell us before?!"

Übung 10: Prepositions. Wähle jeweils die richtige der drei Präpositionen aus!

1. She wore a light pink coloured top *(by/with/on)* .... a necklace and white trousers.

2. She was tapping her *(on/at/for)* .... the shoulder.

3. He was coming *(in/through/by)* .... the door but he wasn't alone.

4. She looked around for him and *(with/from/after)* .... a few minutes, she realized he wasn't there.

5. She came *(from/under/over)* .... to speak *(around/to/by)* .... her.

6. Evie told the others *(around/about/of)* .... her feelings.

Emily responded more quietly, but equally happy, "Well, Eve, this is the best birthday ever! So have you told him how you feel? Why didn't you tell me before, silly?"
Now she came over to where Evie was sitting, gave her a big hug, held her hand and said, "Eve, you obviously really like him. You never talk about boys and you never really mention that you fancy someone unless you have strong feelings for them. So, come on, tell us, how did it happen?"
Evie felt much better having Emily at her side while talking about Nick. She told them the story of how they had met at football practice and that she was too embarrassed to speak to him then.
When Evie finished the story, Emily was very surprised.
"What's that, Eve? You haven't even spoken to him? What? But how can you fancy someone if you don't speak to him? I mean, you need to know the guy first to see what he's like... a good-looking boy isn't everything, you know!"
Evie felt like asking her who she had in mind, but thought it best to leave it until later. She had a feeling who it might be...
Nina agreed with Emily on this.
"Well of course," she said. "Marcus and I got to know each other first and that's why I knew I really liked him, because

equally	genauso, gleichermaßen
obviously	offensichtlich
unless	es sei denn, dass
have sth. in mind	etw. im Sinn haben
to break the silence	das Schweigen brechen
sporty	sportlich

he is funny and he makes me really happy." The girls all looked at Nina with a big smile across their faces. They were all so happy for her – Marcus and Nina looked really good together and they knew that he truly was a nice guy, too.
This time, Holly broke the silence. "Well, exactly. This is why we had to discuss this. Also, I don't know if Nick is really the right guy for you, Eve. He's sporty, that's good, but he has had so many girlfriends. I don't really know if he's right for you, Eve..."

Übung 11: Verb forms. Wie lautet das Simple Past der folgenden Verben?

1. feel ....
2. meet ....
3. come ....
4. brake ....
5. give ....
6. get ....
7. speak ....
8. sit ....

The other two girls disagreed with this, especially Emily, who was determined to support Nick, even though she didn't know him either.
"Well, we don't know that, we're just guessing right now. He seems like a really nice guy and I'm sure Evie would have chosen someone special. But I do think it's very important that Evie gets to know him first."
The girls all nodded their heads. Evie looked at all of them and she realized that she felt a lot better, now that she had talked about her feelings. She didn't feel so alone anymore. Yes, her friends were right, she had to speak to Nick; it was important to get to know him. So even if he had a girlfriend, it was okay to be friends, at least...

to disagree	anderer Meinung sein
determined	entschlossen
to support	befürworten, unterstützen
to guess	raten
fair	Kirmes
at the sound of	beim Hören von

Then, Nina had a great idea, "Well, why don't you ask him out? Not as a boyfriend, but just ask him out for a coffee, so that you can speak to him outside of school?"
Holly nodded and then said, "Yeah, I agree, you need to see him a bit more. Why don't you ask him to take you to the summer fair at the park? You could even go on a boat trip with him across the lake!"
At the sound of Holly's romantic idea, all the girls started laughing, but Evie was already thinking about how to ask Nick to the fair. The girls left Evie's room and went back downstairs together to join the rest of the party.

Übung 12: Hidden words. Finde in dem Suchrätsel acht Wörter aus dem vorhergehenden Textabschnitt!

E	I	D	P	K	O	N	A	I	C	X	A
N	U	Z	R	B	I	R	T	H	D	A	Y
T	R	F	L	I	R	T	I	N	G	R	P
I	P	F	A	G	H	B	C	A	P	O	A
R	R	S	I	F	T	C	P	H	L	Y	R
E	I	V	Y	A	N	U	W	O	E	Q	E
B	N	M	B	O	Y	F	R	I	E	N	D
C	C	I	L	R	Z	H	N	B	P	L	G
A	E	R	O	E	H	G	A	L	A	W	F
F	S	A	N	K	L	X	B	O	Z	N	I
H	S	E	D	S	C	A	R	F	H	J	L
K	A	T	E	M	A	R	Z	O	G	A	K

right on time	zur rechten Zeit
to head towards	zusteuern auf
to wave sb. goodbye	jmd. zum Abschied winken

As if right on time, Evie saw Nick walk into the room and head towards the front door. As he was leaving, he waved her goodbye. She was pretty sure he even smiled at her!

3

Back to School

3

Die Party war ein voller Erfolg! Alle haben sich prächtig amüsiert. Und Evie ist wieder zuversichtlicher: sie muss nur auf die richtige Gelegenheit warten, um Nick zur Kirmes einzuladen.
Doch dann kommt es in der Mittagspause zu einem Streit. Nina lässt ein paar Bemerkungen los, die Evie richtig sauer machen, und schließlich zieht sie auch noch beleidigt ab!
Nun hat Evie nicht nur Liebeskummer, sondern auch noch Krach mit einer ihrer besten Freundinnen!

Over the next few days, the whole school seemed to be talking about the girls' *Bollywood* party. It had been a great success! People came across to Evie to thank her for the party and she was simply delighted about that. Although she was still a little upset about Nick's new 'blonde' girl, she was really happy that everyone had enjoyed her party.
Olly was really pleased, too. He had also started hanging around with Evie's group of friends a bit more and Evie had a feeling it might be because of the conversation he had had with Emily at the party...

The girls were extremely happy, as well. After Evie's confession, the party had continued into the night. Evie had felt more relaxed without Nick there and had enjoyed herself much more. She had even tried out an Indian dance! They had taken many pictures with their digital cameras and the girls said they would look through the photos together at lunchtime.

delighted	hocherfreut
pleased	erfreut, zufrieden
to hang around with sb.	mit jmd. herumhängen
confession	Geständnis
lunchtime	Mittagszeit
bench	Bank
packed lunch	Lunchpaket
to be thrilled	sich wahnsinnig freuen
have the courage to do sth.	den Mut haben, etw. zu tun

Since it was nearly one o'clock, Evie started walking over to the bench where the girls would all meet for lunch. It was a nice day, so they decided to eat their packed lunches outdoors in the sunshine. As she was walking along, she saw her classmate Anna walking towards the school and they both stopped to talk to one another. Evie really liked Anna, because she was always very friendly.

"Hey, Evie! Thank you so much for the great *Bollywood* evening! All my friends thought your party was fantastic and we were just wondering if you were free to come with us to the fair on Saturday?"

Evie was thrilled. But what would she tell her friends, especially because she still hadn't had the courage to invite Nick?! Unfortunately, she would have to say no to Anna's invite, Evie thought.

cheerfully	fröhlich
That was really lucky!	Das war wirklich ein Glück!
thicket of bushes	Gebüsch
to catch up with sb.	jmd. einholen
to finish (off)	erledigen
to hand in	einreichen, abgeben

"Hey, Anna, thank you so much for the invitation. That's a great idea, but Nina, Holly, Emily and I have made plans to go to the fair together! But you and your friends are more than welcome to join us, if you want!"

Anna looked disappointed, but responded cheerfully. "Oh, okay! Don't worry, I'm sure we'll see each other at the fair! Do you know anyone else who's going?"

Evie smiled and said, "Not yet... but I'm pretty sure we'll see lots of people there. I've heard a lot of people talk about the fair. To be honest, I forgot the fair was so soon. I'm glad Emily's birthday was last weekend, because it was definitely the best weekend for the party!"

"Yeah, that was really lucky! Okay, well, I'll let you go and meet your friends – I saw them sitting over there by those benches."

Anna pointed towards a thicket of bushes and a few benches. From where she was standing, Evie could just make out Nina's blonde hair.

"Okay, great! Thank you so much for the invitation, Anna, we'll definitely see each other at the fair!"

"Thanks, Evie. See you soon!" Anna walked towards the school building and left Evie to catch up with her friends.

***Übung 13:** Match-up. Verbinde die Wörter mit ihrer Übersetzung!*

1. Erfolg	invitation
2. erfreut	classmate
3. Geständnis	fair
4. Entscheidung	success
5. Klassenkamerad	courage
6. Einladung	delighted
7. Kirmes	decision
8. Mut	confession

"Guys!" Evie called out to her friends who were sitting around.

Emily seemed to be reading a novel, Nina was checking her make-up – probably because she was seeing Marcus later on – and Holly was busy finishing off some homework she had to hand in after lunch.

"Hey, Eve!" The girls stopped what they were doing to watch their friend running towards them. They waved their arms, and Evie greeted all of them with a quick hug.

"Guys! I've just been speaking to Anna. It looks like the entire group of her friends is going to the fair, too!"

"Really?" Holly said. "I do like Anna and her crowd; they all seem so very friendly!"
"Yeah, and get this – she has invited me to the fair to join all her friends!" Evie said excitedly.
At the sound of this, Nina, Holly and Emily all looked a little disappointed.
"Ah, don't be silly, you lot, I said no, obviously… even though I was tempted to go with them and therefore say no to all of you!" Evie smiled at her friends.
This time, Emily laughed and said, "Ah, Eve, sometimes you are funny. But if you wanted to, you know you could always go with them. It's just… I hope you haven't forgotten about inviting Nick?"
Hearing this, Evie stopped smiling and looked down.
"Yeah, I haven't really had a chance to invite him yet. I was thinking that I could maybe do that tonight, after football practice. I just hope I'm doing the right thing!"
The girls looked sympathetic and Nina started talking.
"You know… you don't have to call him if you don't want to, Evie," she said, finishing off her make-up.
"I do understand that it is difficult to invite someone when they are going out with someone else… For example, I'm not sure what I would think if another girl should ask Marcus to the fair on Saturday…"

crowd	*hier:* Clique
ϟ Get this!	Hör dir das an!
ϟ you lot	ihr da
to be tempted	in Versuchung geraten
sympathetic	mitfühlend

Evie was surprised by the way her friend said this and felt quite hurt. But fortunately, Emily answered while Evie listened silently.
"Well Nina, I think that sounds a bit harsh, don't you think? Eve is hardly 'another girl' to Nick, because they have met each other many times on the football field. He obviously wants to speak to her! After all, there is nothing wrong with being friends with a boy!"

harsh	barsch
to go after sb.	jmd. nachlaufen
behaviour	Benehmen, Verhalten
to guess about sth.	etw. erraten

"Yes, of course, Emily, it is fine to be friends with a boy. But if he already has a girlfriend and you fancy him, too, it is not a good idea to be going after him... Is it fair to say, Emily, that you and Olly are more than just friends?!"
Emily blushed at the sound of this and looked away. She didn't say anything. Evie had to admit that she was a little surprised at Nina's behaviour. They all knew that Olly and Emily were getting quite close. Since Olly was her own brother, she could see that he really liked Emily. Emily was also her best friend and although Emily hadn't told her, Evie had guessed about her best friend's feelings for Olly from the party. But why was Nina being so harsh?
Before Evie or Holly could respond, Nina got up and said, "I have to go and meet Marcus now!" and left.

The girls watched Nina walk away. None of them spoke until their friend entered the school doors.

"What was that all about?!" Holly asked.

She was still trying to understand what had just happened. She had been very quiet during the conversation, because she had to finish her English homework about a Shakespeare play.

"Why do you think she was so upset?" Holly added, while she closed her textbooks and placed her homework in her bag.

"I'm not sure", Evie said, trying her best to sound positive. She was not so sure of what to say to Emily, who had turned bright pink.

Emily was holding the new camera she had got for her birthday and remained silent. Holly could see that she looked really hurt, too. So, to change the conversation, she said:
"Let's look at some of the photos from our party! That will cheer all of us up!"
Emily was happy to do something else and turned on her new camera, so that the three girls could start looking through the photos. Although Evie and Emily were not really in the mood to look at the photographs, some of them were just too funny not to smile about. Especially the photo of Olly – dancing and wearing his turban – was hilarious!

textbook	Lehrbuch
bright	leuchtend
to remain silent	schweigen, nichts sagen
to cheer up	aufheitern, bessere Laune bekommen

At the end of the school day, Evie had to stay behind at school, so that she could go to football practice. But before she went to the football field, she said goodbye to her friends and gave Emily a big hug.

to be in the mood	in Stimmung sein
hilarious	urkomisch
to stay behind	(zurück)bleiben

Übung 14: Crossword. Trage die Lösungen ein!

1. At lunchtime, the girls were sitting on a ...
2. The fair is on this day of the week.
3. The girls are looking at pictures on a ...
4. Olly is Evie's ...
5. Holly is finishing her homework on a play by this famous writer.
6. Evie and Emily were not in the ... to look at the photographs.
7. What is the theme of the fancy-dress birthday party?

"I hope you're not worrying about what Nina said earlier on... about Olly and..."
But Emily quickly changed the conversation to something else.
"Yeah... but more importantly, Eve, I still think you should ask Nick at football practice about Saturday. Just see what he has to say, okay?"
Evie nodded in agreement. But after what Nina had said, she was really confused about whether she should ask him, or not. The two friends said goodbye and Evie started walking towards the girls' changing rooms.

confused	verwirrt
whether	ob
otherwise	ansonsten

On the way, she began to think about Nina. Nina hadn't spoken to any of them, because she had been with Marcus the whole day. After school, the two of them also had made plans to go to the cinema together. But Nina was right. That was the thing that hurt Evie the most... Nina had spoken the truth! Why should she try and become friends with Nick when he already had a girlfriend? Evie still wasn't sure whether or not that girl was his girlfriend, but who could she otherwise be? None of them knew her name and no-one at school had ever seen her before...

Übung 15: Match-up. Was denkt Evie?

1.	Nina hadn't spoken	could be Nick's girlfriend.
2.	Nina was	had seen her before.
3.	Nina has spoken	right.
4.	The girl	the truth.
5.	No-one	the girl's name.
6.	Nobody knows	to any of them.

Full of confusion, Evie entered the changing rooms. Now she had to think about the football match. She couldn't think about Nick, Nina, or anyone else. She had to concentrate on football, because today, the girls' team was to be chosen for the match in a few weeks' time.

She put on her football shirt, tracksuit bottoms and football boots. She placed a sweatband on her wrist and set off towards the football field to join the rest of her team. She was already running quite late and Evie knew that her coach would be quite angry. As she had predicted... her coach was furious!

"Evie Smith! Where have you been? Get a move on and run around the field five times! GO!" The coach blew his whistle.

Evie tried to catch up with the rest of her team, but they had nearly finished by now. When she was done, football practice had already begun. So Evie had to sit on the benches to wait her turn. Her coach came up to Evie in the middle of the match and spoke to her.

tracksuit bottoms	Trainings-hose
sweatband	Schweißband
wrist	Handgelenk
to set off	sich auf den Weg machen
to predict	voraussagen
whistle	Trillerpfeife
done	fertig
to wait one's turn	warten, bis man an der Reihe ist

Übung 16: Odd one out! Welches Wort passt nicht in die Reihe?

1. football, football shirt, tracksuit bottoms, football boots
2. funny, happy, disappointed, excited
3. dissatisfied, angry, furious, smiling
4. sweet, odd, nice, lovely
5. classmate, teacher, boss, coach
6. run, jog, sit, go
7. wrist, arm, elbow, head
8. stay behind, set off, wait one's turn, remain

perform-ance	Leistung
attacker	Angreifer(in)
distracted	unaufmerksam, abgelenkt
dissatisfied	unzufrieden
to score a goal	ein Tor schießen
to pat sb. on the back	jmd. auf die Schulter klopfen
Keep it up!	Mach weiter so!

"Evie, I'm very pleased with your performance within the team. You're a strong attacker and I know you've got what I need for the match in a couple of weeks. But lately, you seem a little distracted. Do you mind if I ask what's wrong?"
Evie didn't say much in return.

"No, sir, everything is fine. I'm just a little tired today, that's all. Do you think I could join the rest of the team for the second-half?"
He looked dissatisfied with her answer, but allowed her to join the team after the break. Evie played brilliantly and scored two goals. She was so happy, she completely forgot about Nick and the trouble with Nina earlier that afternoon. At the end of practice, the coach came up to her again and patted her on the back.
"That's much better, my girl, keep it up!"

Übung 17: Contracted forms. Wie heißt die Kurzform?

1. I cannot ....
2. I am ....
3. you did not ....
4. you are ....
5. we will ....
6. you do not ....
7. let us ....
8. they are ....

Evie beamed with joy. She jogged over to the benches to pick up her water bottle and sports kit and didn't even notice who was sitting on one of the benches.

"Hey, Evie!"

It was Nick. She turned around to see him in his football shorts and football shirt. He looked very muddy.

"I watched you play some great football there! You really know how to get those goals, don't you? Maybe we could practise together sometime?"

Evie smiled, but was still too shy to say 'yes' directly to him.

to beam with joy	vor Freude strahlen
to pick up	aufheben, mitnehmen
muddy	schmutzig, veschlammt
to stammer	stammeln, stottern
to build up one's courage	seinen Mut sammeln

"I was wondering, actually... umm... what you were doing this weekend?" he asked.

At the sound of this, Evie cheered up and spoke to him.

"I-I-I'm not doing much, I-I don't think."

Evie was quite nervous and started to stammer a little. She was so shocked to find him waiting for her at the benches and now he was asking her what she was doing this weekend! She realized that she sounded a little silly, so she quickly built up more courage to continue to speak to him.

"Yeah, actually... my friends and I were planning to go to the fair... So I was wondering if..."

By now, Evie had picked up her sports kit and walked across to him. Nick stood up quickly and the two of them started talking on the football field.

The rest of her team had already gone into the changing rooms, but her coach gave her a big grin before he walked towards the school building.

"That's great, 'cos I was thinking of going, too! Do you want us to go together... or, what I mean is... maybe you could meet me there?"

Evie couldn't believe what she was hearing. Nick had come up to speak to her and now he was trying to invite her to the fair! This was incredible. She had the biggest smile on her face.

"Of course, that would be great! You could meet my friends, too and..."

ϟ 'cos	Kurzform von „because"
excitement	Begeisterung
by the looks of things	*hier:* so wie es aussah
hastily	hastig
excuse	Ausrede
dodgems	Autoscooter

Suddenly she remembered Nina's comments. In her excitement, she had forgotten all about his girlfriend and, by the looks of things, he had forgotten all about her, too.

He looked a little confused when she stopped talking.

"Is everything okay?"

"Yeah, I'm fine... I just... I was just thinking about the... about the... about your... about the time we should meet!" Evie responded hastily.

She had very little time to think of a good excuse for her silence. She just didn't have the courage to mention his girlfriend... yet.

"Oh, yeah, of course..." Nick replied, "I completely forgot about that! Let's say around seven, near the dodgems? They're always a pretty big thing at the fair!"

Übung 18: Choose the right word!
Setze das passende Adjektiv ein.

jealous *embarrassed* *muddy* *biggest*

strong *tall* *surprised* *great*

1. Sometimes the football field can be ....
2. A person who feels uncomfortable is ....
3. She was .... on her birthday.
4. Football players are usually quite ....
5. A person who is happy feels ....
6. A girl who sees her boyfriend talk to another girl is ....
7. Evie had the .... smile on her face.
8. A .... blonde-haired girl is waiting for Nick.

"Okay, at seven at the dodgems", she said shyly.
"Cool! Well, it was really good to see you, Evie, but I actually need to go now, because I'm... umm... meeting someone after football practice! So, we'll say seven at the dodgems? I think Nina's got my number, so you can call me on that if we get lost!"
Before she could respond, he had jogged off to meet 'someone'. In the distance, Evie could see a tall blonde-haired girl waiting near the school entrance. Maybe he hadn't forgotten about her at all...

4

Misunder-standings

4

Warum hat Nina nicht gesagt, dass sie Nicks Telefonnummer hat? Evies Vertrauen zur ihrer Freundin ist erschüttert. Zwischen ihnen herrscht erst einmal Funkstille, und auch das Treffen mit Nick auf der Kirmes läuft nicht so wie geplant. Evie ist total enttäuscht: Wahrscheinlich hatte Nina doch recht, und sie hat sich alles nur eingebildet. Emily versucht, ihre Freundin zu trösten, doch plötzlich ist Evie in der Menge verschwunden. Muss Emily sich ernsthaft Sorgen um sie machen?

"Why didn't you tell me you had Nick's number?" Evie was not pleased. The meeting with Nick the evening before had been unexpected. She was surprised that he invited her to the fair, but she was even more surprised by what he had said as he was leaving. Nina had his number, which meant that the two of them were in contact with each other. But why hadn't Nina just told her that before? Evie looked at her now, and continued to talk.

"Honestly, Nina, I don't understand. You yell at me for trying to be friends with him but, from what I can see, you've been in contact with him all this time and you didn't even tell me...!"

Evie was really hurt. She knew she might be overreacting, but she didn't care right now. She hadn't slept all night, because she kept thinking about how silly she must have looked standing alone on the football field after Nick had left.

Why did he have to speak with her? Why couldn't he just have gone out with the blonde-haired girl and left her alone?

It was really annoying Evie that, for the first time, she was getting upset over a guy! She was behaving like all the other girls she used to laugh about with Emily!

Evie wasn't like the other girls. She was different and just liked to be friends with boys.

Lots of boys had shown an interest in her at school, but she never really liked any of them for one reason or another. This was the very first time she wasn't friends with a boy and yet had strong feelings for him. She felt ridiculous. But the four people she knew she could always trust were Olly, Emily, Holly and Nina. All she could think about now was that Nick had given Nina his number.

unexpected	unerwartet
to yell at sb.	jmd. anschreien
to overreact	überreagieren
ridiculous	lächerlich
to get attention from sb.	jmd. auffallen, von jmd. beachtet werden

Nina was one of the prettiest girls at school. She always got attention from boys.

Evie hadn't really noticed this before but, this time, things were different.

to turn back	umkehren
tear	Träne
unaware	nichts ahnend, unwissend
mess	Chaos, Durcheinander
to drift apart	auseinander gehen

"Evie, I don't know why you are getting so upset... he gave me his number ages ago!"
"Well, to be honest, Nina, I don't know what to say... I just don't understand why you had to keep it a secret from me. I didn't even know that you were friends with him! It makes me think that you didn't want me to contact him 'cos you fancy him yourself! You told us at the party that you think he's really good-looking, didn't you?! So why don't you just leave Marcus and go out with Nick instead?!"
With that, Evie walked away. She walked on and didn't turn back to see the tears on Nina's face.

School continued normally that day, but the girls' friendship had completely changed. Nina and Evie were no longer speaking to each other. Since it was Friday, they were all meant to go to the fair together the next day. Emily and Holly were confused about what to do. They couldn't choose between their friends but, in the end, they decided to go separately. Holly could take Nina to the fair and Emily would join Evie. However, the drama didn't stop there.
Unaware of her friends' plans, Nina no longer wanted to go to the fair at all and Evie was thinking of going with Anna and her friends! It was a complete mess and Emily felt quite sad that they were all slowly drifting apart. Whatever would happen tomorrow?

***Übung 19:** Unscramble the sentences! Was wirft Evie ihrer Freundin Nina vor? Bilde sinnvolle Sätze mit den durcheinander geratenen Wörtern.*

1. all the time – with Nick – You – in contact – have been.

....

2. boys – You – from – get attention – always.

....

3. friends – Nick – You – are – and.

....

4. didn't – You – to contact – want me – him.

....

5. yourself – Nick – You – fancy!

....

6. Nick's number – tell me – you – had – You didn't!

....

7. friends – a secret – You – that – kept it – you are.

....

to pick up the phone	den Hörer abnehmen
ϟ mate	Kumpel, Freund

On Saturday, Emily phoned Nina in the afternoon to see if she was okay, but Nina didn't answer the phone. She then tried Marcus' number and he, too, didn't answer his phone. Maybe they were together. She tried Evie, who eventually picked up the phone.

"Hello, is that Eve?"
"Hey, Em..."
"Are you okay today?"
"Yeah... fine... just about... do you think I was too harsh to Nina? She's really upset with me, isn't she?"
"To be honest, I haven't spoken to her. She's not answering the phone. I tried Marcus, too, but his phone just goes to voicemail. How are you feeling anyway?"
"Yeah..., great."
"Okay... well, do you still want to go to the fair?"
"Yeah, well, I kind of have to, don't I? Now that Nick's decided that he wants to be mates..."
"Eve... I know you're annoyed from your conversation with him, but please try and see the

bigger picture. He waited for you at the football field and he has invited you to the fair…; those are fairly big steps for a guy to take. There must be something there!"

to see the bigger picture	das Ganze sehen
fairly	ziemlich
fool	Dummkopf, Narr
ϟ not that much of a big deal	keine so große Sache
odd	merkwürdig
to rush off	(davon)eilen

"Yeah, maybe… but to then find out that him and Nina are in contact – 'Oh, just give me a call from Nina's mobile!' – I mean, he didn't even stop to give me the number himself! I still have to contact him through Nina, which just makes me look like a fool!"

"I knew that was the problem, Eve! I knew it was because he didn't give you his number himself. But it's really not that much of a big deal! I mean, I've asked guys for their number before and they didn't think it was odd that I asked. But didn't you say that he was rushing off somewhere?"

"Umm… yes… to see his girlfriend!"

to giggle	kichern
to make up one's mind	sich entscheiden
eyelashes	Wimpern
to kid	scherzen

At this point, the two girls started giggling and laughing at the ridiculous situation on the phone. Evie felt better for speaking to Emily and told her that she would go to the fair with her. She still felt quite sad that Nina was hurt and she made up her mind to talk to Nina at the fair.

The afternoon went by very quickly, until there was only half an hour left for Evie to get ready. She ran upstairs, put on some jeans and a nice sparkly top and sat down to do her make-up. She wore her new eye shadow, put on some pretty earrings, quickly brushed her eyelashes with mascara and picked up her lip gloss before going downstairs. On the way, she saw Olly.
He smiled when he saw her. "Wow! So where is the lady going?!"
"Off to the fair... but how come you're not going?!"
"Ah. I've got things to do around the house. I'll see how I feel later on though... why, are you going to miss me?"
Olly smiled as he said this, but Evie didn't laugh. She seemed quite serious.
"Yeah, actually, Olly, ... are you sure you can't come?"
"You okay, Eve? I was only kidding! But if you want, I'll see if I can go later on. I had plans to meet some of the guys at seven," Olly replied.

"Oh, okay! No, don't worry, Olly, you go and have a good time!" With that, Evie gave him a kiss on the cheek and left.

Übung 20: A phone call. Bringe den Dialog zwischen Evie und Emily in die richtige Reihenfolge!

a) Yeah, well, I kind of have to, don't I?

b) Hello, is that Eve?

c) Yeah... fine... How are you feeling anyway?

d) Are you okay today?

e) Hey, Em...

f) Yes, you're right. Let's meet at the entrance at half past six!

g) Okay... well, do you still want to go to the fair?

1	2	3	4	5	6	7

Emily was going to meet her near the park, but Evie was already running a bit late. Although she was running late, she decided to walk to the park as it was only ten minutes away. As she was walking, she felt quite nervous about the meeting with Nick. What would he say? Now she was a little unsure about this 'friendship'. Nina was right. He had a girlfriend, so what was she doing?

Emily had seen Evie from a distance and began to walk towards her friend. She hugged her and took her by the hand.

"Come on, you, cheer up! We'll go on the dodgems, have some candyfloss and then you can meet Nick. Where are we meeting him again?"

Evie loved her friend's enthusiasm, even when things were not going so well.
"The dodgems," she answered.
"The dodgems! Fantastic! I'm sure he will be happy to see you, especially because you're looking stunning tonight!"
Evie grumbled, but didn't really say much. She walked with Emily and soon they entered the fairground.

It was packed! There were teenagers, parents with kids and plenty of pupils from their school! She saw Anna in the distance and waved.
Anna smiled and waved back. She was waiting with three of her other friends in the queue for a ride and they looked like they were all having so much fun! When Evie saw them, she felt quite sad. It was all her fault. If she hadn't yelled at Nina, the four of them would happily be going to the fair and everything would be just fine. Emily seemed to read her mind and she squeezed Evie's hand gently.

to be running late	sich verspäten
Cheer up!	Kopf hoch!
candyfloss	Zuckerwatte
enthusiasm	Begeisterung
to look stunning	umwerfend aussehen
to grumble	grummeln, murren
fairground	Festplatz
packed	überfüllt
to wave	winken
queue	Schlange
to squeeze	drücken

Übung 21: Match-up. Verbinde die passenden Ausdrücke!

1. buy	away
2. read	make-up
3. wore	candyfloss
4. put on	football
5. play	the fairground
6. walk	her mind
7. enter	for a ride
8. queue	earrings

"Eve, it's fine... come on, let's go and find Nick. It's almost seven!"
They slowly walked over to the dodgems. From the distance, Evie could see that there was a huge queue. It would be quite difficult to find Nick in the crowd. But suddenly, there he was: the tall, broad-shouldered Nick that all the fuss was about.
They walked over to him and Evie could see Emily's walk turn into small skips of joy... at least one of them was excited about the meeting! When Nick spotted them, he, too, started to walk towards them and soon they were talking.

"Hey, girls, how are you both? Seems like a good fair to me!"
"Yeah, it is!" Emily squealed with joy.
"Hey, Evie!" Having noticed her silence, Nick said hello again.
"Hi," she replied, but her reply was very short, polite, and not particularly friendly. Nick didn't seem to be too bothered.
"So... umm... do you guys want to go on the dodgems? We can split up into pairs. Oh, I forgot to say, there's someone I want you both to meet! She'll be here any second. Are your other mates coming, too?"
Evie couldn't believe it. She just knew that they were about to meet his girlfriend and now he was wondering where Nina was!
Emily also felt surprised by what he had just said. Before either of them could answer, they saw the blonde girl walking towards them. Even Evie had to admit that she was an extremely pretty girl.
As she approached them, Evie thought the girl seemed quite shy and modest. She even seemed really friendly!
"Ah. There she is... Louise!" Nick called out to her and then he looked towards Evie.

ϟ fuss	Aufregung
skip of joy	Freudensprung
to squeal	(auf)jubeln
particularly	besonders
either of them	eine(r) von beiden
to approach	sich nähern, herankommen
modest	bescheiden

"Evie, I want to introduce you to my..."

But before he could even finish the sentence, Evie interrupted him.

"Oh, Nick, I'm so sorry but, I'm afraid, we're going to have to leave. We told the others we would meet them at ten past seven and we're already running a bit late... umm... we'll catch up with you some other time! Say hi to umm... Louise from me and tell her we're really sorry!" Before he could answer, Evie grabbed Emily's arm and they rushed away. She was walking so fast that neither of them could even hear Nick trying to stop them. When they were at a safe distance, Evie let go of Emily's arm which had turned bright red from Evie's strong grip.

"Eve! What was that all about?"

"I'm sorry, Em, I can't, I just can't..."

"Whatever is the matter with you, Evie? He was just about to introduce us to whoever this Louise is! After all, we're simply guessing that they're going out!"

"Em, seriously, I really appreciate you trying to help me out, but I'm fine. Anyway, I've given up on the idea of Nick now. Nina was so right! What

to introduce sb.	jmd. vorstellen
ϟ We'll catch up with you some other time!	Wir sehen uns demnächst!
to grab	greifen
neither of them	keine(r) von ihnen
safe	sicher, gefahrlos
to let go of sth.	etw. loslassen
grip	Griff
Whatever is the matter?	Was ist denn los?
to appreciate sth.	dankbar sein (für etw.)

was I thinking? I'm such an idiot. He obviously has a girlfriend and she looked so lovely, I can't do that to her either. Okay, I was a little rude, but I just didn't want to meet her. I just couldn't, Em..."

Evie looked a little tearful. The truth was that she just didn't know him at all and it was best to leave it at that.

Emily didn't know what to say. She looked at her friend and remained silent. This was turning into the worst evening ever.

"Well, Evie, Holly did actually want to meet up with us. She just sent me a text message. Maybe we should go and see her – then you might feel a little better! I don't think Nina's with her, but I can't be sure."

rude	unhöflich, ruppig
tearful	weinerlich

"No, no. You go ahead. I might just walk back home now. I don't really want to make it a bad night for everyone."

"You wouldn't, Eve, we're all here for you, and..."

"In fact, Em, just go, I need to be on my own for a bit. You guys have been amazing and I've just ruined my friendship with Nina. I don't want to say anything else that might make the situation worse."

"Listen, Evie, why..."

But before Emily could even finish her sentence, Evie had already started to walk away. Emily wanted to follow her but, suddenly, her phone rang. It was Holly and so she answered it.

"Hey, Holly!"

"Hey, Em! Whereabouts are you guys? Nina's here with me. To be honest, I made sure she came with me to the fair! She really doesn't mind if Evie's there either!"

***Übung 22:** Unscramble the words!*
Ordne die Buchstaben so, dass sich ein sinnvolles Wort ergibt.

1. GEDDOMS ....
2. FLANDYCOSS ....
3. GRUNFODAIR ....
4. NEERTAGES ....
5. CISUM ....
6. STHIGL ....
7. NAGIZAM ....

Emily just remembered Evie and turned around to see a massive crowd! Where was she?
"Oh, my goodness, Holly, I think I've just lost her!"
"You've lost who?! What's going on?"

"Listen, I'll tell you when you're here. Meet me by the candyfloss stand in five minutes – we need to find Evie. I'll tell you what happened when we meet.... I can't really hear you with all this noise!"
"Okay, Em, we'll be there immediately!"
The girls met at the candyfloss stand and Emily explained the situation. Nina was the first to react.
"Oh, no! She must be so upset! Have you tried ringing her mobile?"
"Well, I tried ringing her after our conversation, but she's not answering. I just hope she walked home!" Emily looked very concerned.
"Well, you've got Olly's number, right? Try and give him a ring and see if she is back at home by now!" Holly suggested.

ϟ whereabouts	wo etwa
massive crowd	große Menschenmenge
candyfloss stand	Zuckerwattestand
concerned	besorgt
to suggest	vorschlagen
weird	seltsam

"Yeah, actually that's a really good idea. I'll give him a call right now!", Emily answered and, this time, she didn't feel so weird talking about Olly in front of her friends.
"Olly?"
"Em, hi! How are you?"
"I'm fine! Listen, is Evie there?"
"Umm, no! I thought she was with all of you?"
"No, she isn't... we've kind of lost her. Do you think you could come over to the fair? She'll definitely listen to you if you call her."

to queue up	Schlange stehen
toffee apples	kandierte Äpfel
teacups	Teetassen (-Karussell)

"Lost her?!"
"Yeah. I just turned around for a second and she was gone! I thought she would come back, but then my phone rang and afterwards I couldn't see her in the huge crowd. I called her just now, but she's not answering. I don't know if she can hear it or if she's just ignoring me..."
"She wanted me to come to the fair! I knew she wasn't in a good mood when she left the house. I'll be there in ten minutes. Where do you want to meet?"
"Brilliant! Meet us by the candyfloss stand – we'll wait for you there. It's right beside the main entrance."
"Okay, no problem, I'll give her a call on the way and I'll look out for her in case she is walking back! See ya soon, bye!"

The girls stood there and waited. They were all very quiet as they watched people queuing up to buy candyfloss and toffee apples from the stand. Although they were all very hungry, none of them were in the mood to eat. Finally, they saw Olly walking across the field.
"Girls! I've found her – she's standing near the teacups ride!"
"Oh, thank goodness!" Emily said, giving Olly a big hug in front of Holly and Nina.
The girls smiled and so did Olly. They quickly walked over to the ride where they spotted her. Evie was watching the

Übung 23: I've lost her! Bringe Emilys Bericht in die richtige Reihenfolge.

a) I called her just now.

b) I thought she would come back.

c) Afterwards I couldn't see her in the huge crowd.

d) I turned around for a second.

e) But than my phone rang.

f) She isn't answering.

g) Then she was gone.

1	2	3	4	5	6	7

ϟ to scream and shout	herumtoben
to spin round	herumwirbeln
pleasantly surprised	angenehm überrascht
pathetic	jämmerlich, erbärmlich
to delete	löschen
pat	Klaps

girls and boys screaming and shouting with joy, as the teacups spun them round and round. Emily walked up to her and gently tapped her on the shoulder.

"Eve, are you okay?" she asked.

Evie turned around and was pleasantly surprised when she saw Emily, Olly, Holly and Nina looking at her. She smiled at Emily, but first went up to Nina.

"Nina, I'm so sorry about everything. You were right all along. It's fine to be just friends with Nick, really it is, I don't mind any more! I realize now that I was being really pathetic!"

"Ah, Evie, don't be so silly. I was wrong. I deleted his number after we spoke and I promise, I really wanted it to work out between you two. I was just worried about you, that's all!"
The two girls made up and hugged one another. Emily and Holly started cheering and the girls quickly made Evie feel much better.
Olly gave his sister a pat on the back and said, "Well, who wants to go on the teacups with me?"

Übung 24: Fill in the right words! Setze die richtigen Wörter ein und finde das Lösungswort heraus.

1. Teddybär .... ▮ ....
2. Telefon .... ▮ ....
3. Zuckerwatte .... ▮ ....
4. Mädchen ▮ ....
5. Ereignis ▮ ....
6. Stimmung ▮ ....
7. Teetassen .... ▮

Lösung: ....

eventful	erlebnisreich

After the teacups, they went on the dodgems, they then had some candyfloss, won a huge teddy bear and even went on the boat ride! At the end of their eventful evening, even Evie had to admit that the five of them had had a brilliant time!

5

Last Chance for a First Date

5

Endlich eine Sorge weniger! Evie ist überglücklich, dass zwischen ihr und Nina wieder alles in Ordnung ist. Zusammen mit Evies Bruder Olly schauen die vier Mädchen sich die letzten Fotos an. Evie ist froh, dass niemand mehr Nick erwähnt, und genießt die Zeit mit ihren Freundinnen.
Als wieder ihr Fußballtraining ansteht, ist sie sich unschlüssig darüber, wie sie sich gegenüber Nick verhalten soll. Eigentlich will sie ihn gar nicht wiedersehen, aber das wird wohl kaum zu vermeiden sein. Als sie ihn schließlich nach dem Training trifft, ist es wieder er, der sie anspricht …

Another week had begun for Evie, Emily, Holly and Nina. But at least now they were all speaking to each other again. At school, the girls were eating their lunch and talking about their favourite moments at the fair. Olly had taken them around the fair and the girls had really appreciated that. However, Evie felt quite sad about her situation with Nick. But her friends had made sure that they didn't speak about him and she was grateful for that.
After school, they all met at Evie's house to look through the photos from the *Bollywood* night and the fair. Emily

had taken many photos at the fair and Nina hadn't yet seen the pictures from the party. This time, Evie and Emily both felt happy to look through the photos. Olly joined them, too.

"Oh, look at this one! Evie's on the ride with Holly and Holly's hair is all over the place!", Nina said, looking at the photo and laughing.

"Let's have a look," Holly mumbled in a worried voice. She didn't really like photos taken of herself.

"Ha-ha!" Evie said, looking at the picture of herself and Holly on the fairground ride.

The girls were lucky that the weather was nice, because they could look at the photos while enjoying the hot sunshine outside in Evie's garden.

to mumble	murmeln, brummeln
fairground ride	Karussell
to be disappointed in sb.	von jmd. enttäuscht sein

It was Monday, so Evie had to leave her friends to go to football practice again. In the few weeks leading up to the match, the team had to practice on Mondays too now. Olly said he would look after the other friends, so Evie went to the school football field. But she walked very slowly, because she was thinking about what to say to Nick. She knew that Nick would be there, too, but she didn't really want to see him. A part of her didn't even want to go to football practice, yet she had to go, because otherwise her coach would be very disappointed in her.

Übung 25: How is Evie feeling after the fair? Ergänze die Sätze und finde heraus, wie Evie sich fühlt.

enjoys | not really want | happy | doesn't know | quite sad

1. Evie feels .... about the situation with Nick.
2. She feels .... to look through the pictures with her friends.
3. She .... to be outside in the sunny garden.
4. She .... what she should say to Nick.
5. She does .... to see him.

When Evie arrived, she didn't see Nick and she felt better about the whole thing. She quickly got ready in the changing rooms and joined her team. The girls' team practised goals, ran several times around the field and the coach taught them several game tactics for the match. So, at the end of football practice, the girls were all very tired.

Just as Evie was walking away from the changing rooms, she saw him: Nick was there, leaning against a wall with his arms crossed. When he saw her, he stood up straight and walked towards her. She was still wearing her sweaty football shirt, but he didn't seem to mind. As he walked towards her, he just kept looking directly into her eyes.

"Evie," he said very softly.

"Hey, Nick," she said.

She tried to walk past, but then he did something very strange. He held her hand to stop her. She quickly turned around, but felt very strange about him holding her hand. Although she was still annoyed with him, his strong firm grip warmed her, but she quickly let go.

"Sorry, Evie. Listen... Actually... I wanted to speak to you. I watched your team practice again. You guys look like you're all in pretty good shape for the match! The coach really makes you work hard. I don't think the boys' team is that fit for the match."

game tactic	taktischer Spielzug
to lean against	lehnen an/gegen
firm grip	fester Griff
in pretty good shape	ziemlich gut in Form

"Thanks. So what did you want to speak to me about?"

This time, he noticed that she was not very friendly and he realized that she was quite annoyed.

"Umm. It was actually about the other night..."

Evie put her sports bag down on the ground and thought that she should at least listen to him. She looked at him, but didn't say anything. So Nick continued to speak.

"Yeah, I kinda just wanted to explain something to you. Just in case you were wondering, I think you should know that Louise isn't my girlfriend. She's my cousin from America."

When she heard that, Evie didn't know what to do or say. What an idiot she was! Emily had been right! They should have really found out about this! She thought back to all the moments she had felt jealous when she had seen Nick and his 'girlfriend' talking together. And all this time, that same girl was actually his cousin!

"Your cousin?!" she shouted out in confusion.

"Yep... my cousin. I think a few people thought she was my girlfriend, because we were spending a lot of time together. She's new to the town and since she doesn't really know anyone here... I thought you and your friends could get to know her and take her around the place. To be honest, I think she's getting pretty bored of me!"

ϟ kinda (kind of)	irgendwie
ϟ yep	ja; jo
mean	gemein, böse
sweet	süß, lieb

At this point, he laughed and Evie laughed with him. In fact, she didn't really know what to say. She was so happy but, more than that, she also felt really silly. She had nearly lost Nina as a friend and she had been mean to Nick. She also felt bad about Louise who must have felt quite hurt when they didn't say hello to her at the fair.

Evie looked at Nick and just wanted to hug him. He looked so sweet and kind as he was talking. Maybe he really did like her and she just didn't think that a guy like him could like a sporty girl like her.

Übung 26: Complete the sentences! Vervollständige die Sätze und finde heraus, was es mit Louise auf sich hat!

1. Evie has a ▯ .... on Nick.
2. She thinks that Nick is in .... ▯ .... with the blonde girl.
3. Evie feels .... ▯ .... about this.
4. She knows the girl's name is .... ▯ .... .
5. She doesn't want to go to football .... ▯ ....
6. Nick wants to speak with her about the other ▯ ....

Louise is Nick's .... !

"Nick, I... I really don't know what to say. I actually thought she was your girlfriend. And I thought..."
"You thought it was best to leave me alone? Yeah, that's what most people did. But I don't understand that even if she was my girlfriend, why did people not speak to me? I'm kind of scared of having a girlfriend now, because everyone might just ignore me again!"

Evie looked down when he said that. She had been one of those people. He must have been hurt by Evie, too.
"I'm really sorry, Nick. I just didn't really want... want to get in the way."
This time, she blushed and she looked at him.
Nick had realized what she meant. He walked towards her and said, "To be honest, Evie, I kinda wish you had got in the way..."
Now he smiled at her.

to get in the way	in die Quere kommen
final	Finale

Evie looked up at him. Nick was standing so close to her, she could smell the aftershave on his neck. He was in his football shirt and jogging bottoms, too, and yet he smelt so good...
Evie quickly stepped back and blushed even more.
"Actually, Evie, I wanted to ask you something. Do you want to go see the football match with me this weekend? I don't know if you like them or not, but the Rangers are playing against the Rovers in the final on Saturday. Do you want to go?"
Evie couldn't believe it. He was inviting her to watch the football match that Olly had been trying to get tickets for! The Rangers were her favourite football team! Well, going to a football match together with Nick... that was more than Evie could ever have wished for on their first date.
"Are you joking?! I love the Rangers! Are you sure? I mean... my brother has been trying to get tickets for weeks!"

"Yeah, well, I thought you might like it. I got tickets for me and Louise, but she really hates football. I thought it would be nice to ask you..."

Evie beamed with joy. The two of them started talking about their favourite football teams. The Rangers were his favourite team, too! They started discussing sport and the two of them couldn't stop talking on the football field...

***Übung 27:** Match-up. Verbinde die Gegenteilpaare miteinander!*

1.	laugh	less
2.	sporty	together
3.	more	cry
4.	scared	frustrated
5.	thrilled	courageous
6.	alone	unathletic
7.	hate	first
8.	final	love

Over the next few days, Evie told her friends everything about her and Nick's conversation. She was telling Emily about it for the fourth time on Friday night. Emily had come round to her house to help her choose an outfit for her date with Nick.

"...and then, Em, he said he thought it would be nice to ask me to the match!"

"Yes, Eve, I know!" But Emily smiled as she said that. She was really happy for Evie. It was brilliant news to find out that Louise was Nick's cousin. And now, all they had to do was to think of the right outfit for tomorrow...

fancy	schick
to Evies's (house)	bei/zu Evie
secretly	heimlich, insgeheim

"You know, Em, I was thinking that maybe I should just wear my football shirt and jeans. I'd feel comfortable in them. I don't think it would be a good idea to wear fancy clothes to a football match!"

Emily had already thought about this and she knew, too, that the football shirt would be the best idea. She had come round to Evie's because she had also secretly been hoping to see Olly... but Olly had gone out with a few of his mates. But Emily was also happy to help her best friend. Evie looked quite nervous, so Emily tried to reassure her.

"Well, Eve, I agree. the Rangers football shirt is the best idea. Maybe, just put on a bit of make-up and it will look perfect!"

"Oh, Em, you're the best and you were right all along!"

Evie now walked over to sit beside her friend.

"But what do you think people at school will say? Holly said that rumours had already started about Nick and me!"

Emily rolled her eyes and said, "Don't think about what other people at our school say. All I know is that Holly, Nina and I are really happy for you. Nina even told me at lunchtime today that she felt bad for doubting Nick before. She's really happy for you both. We all think it's really sweet that he's taking you to the football match!"

Evie looked extremely pleased.

"Thanks, Em... I just hope everything works out with him tomorrow. It's kind of my last chance for a first date!"

The next day, Evie put on her football shirt, jeans and trainers. Evie didn't look as if she was going on a date, she looked sporty and she felt like being herself. She said a quick goodbye to Olly and left to catch the bus. It was raining a little, but she hoped the match would still be good!

rumour	Gerücht
to roll one's eyes	mit den Augen rollen
to doubt sb.	jmd. misstrauen
trainers	Turnschuhe

Übung 28: Odd one out! Welches Wort passt nicht in die Reihe?

1. told, telling, tell, thought
2. crush, boy, guy, mate
3. make-up, mascara, eyelashes, eye-shadow
4. happy, uneasy, lucky, pleased
5. cousin, friend, aunt, sibling
6. reassure, agree, doubt, compromise

Nick had arranged to meet her at the front entrance of the football stadium. It was a twenty-five minute bus ride from where Evie lived, so she listened to her MP3 player on the way to the stadium. She was feeling quite nervous and hoped that the music would calm her.
Evie thought about how happy her friends had been when she had told them about Louise and her first date with Nick. But what if things didn't work out between them? What if he thought she was not the right girl for him after all? But Emily had given her some really good advice last night, so she stopped panicking, closed her eyes and listened to her music for the rest of the journey.
Finally, the bus arrived at the stadium and Evie got off to find many fans dressed in red for the Rangers, just like herself. She suddenly realized that it would be pretty difficult

to find Nick in this crowd! What if he didn't come? But, just as she started to panic, she felt a pat on her shoulder and turned around. There he was, standing in exactly the same football shirt as hers.
"Hey, Evie! Glad to see we've both chosen the same outfit!"
"Yeah, tell me about it! But how did you find me?"
"I was waiting by the bus stop. I thought the front entrance would be too crowded and I wouldn't be able to find you. So I came over here ten minutes ago."
She smiled and he smiled back. They talked a bit more and then, as the match was about to begin, the two of them rushed off into the stadium. While they were walking, he had to hold her hand, so that they didn't lose each other in the crowd... but Evie didn't really mind that at all!

stadium	Stadion
to calm sb.	jmd. beruhigen
advice	Ratschlag
to panic	panisch werden
ϟ Tell me about it!	Wem sagst du das!
referee	Schiedsrichter
score	Spielstand
half-time	Halbzeit
even	*hier:* unentschieden

They had good seats near the front and sat down while Evie looked around. The people in the crowd were dressed in both blue for Rovers FC and red for the Rangers. The atmosphere in the stadium was fantastic and soon the match was about to begin.
The referee blew the whistle and the match began. Both teams were playing extremely well and so the score at half-time was even. During half-time, Nick went to get

some drinks for the two of them. He came back with only one large cola, so they had to drink from the same paper cup.

stall	Verkaufsstand

"Hope that's okay, Evie," he said. "The drinks were pretty expensive at the stall, so I thought it might be good to share!"

"No, that's fine, Nick, I don't mind at all!"

And the two of them smiled at each other again.

__Übung 29:__ Match-up. Verbinde die Wörter mit der passenden Übersetzung!

1. trainers	Stadion
2. sporty	Eingang
3. stadium	Schiedsrichter
4. entrance	Halbzeit
5. match	Spielstand
6. referee	unentschieden
7. team	Turnschuhe
8. score	Spiel
9. half-time	sportlich
10. even	Mannschaft

The match continued, but neither Rangers nor Rovers scored another goal, so the crowd was tense. Everyone thought the match would end in a draw. Now with only two minutes of the match left to go, a striker of the Rangers team had control of the ball and scored a fantastic goal in the last minute! The referee blew the whistle a final time

tense	angespannt, nervös
draw	Unentschieden
striker	Stürmer

and Rangers had won the match! The Rangers players cried out with joy and all the fans started to cheer and shout for them.

Nick and Evie were thrilled! The two of them had been holding hands during the last ten minutes... When Rangers scored the final goal, they had both screamed with joy and hugged each other in the middle of the stands! They were both so happy! They hugged each other for a very long time and eventually they both let go.

"Sorry, Evie... but what a match!"

"Yeah! It was amazing!"

Evie had loved every minute of the match. She had been holding hands with Nick and cheering for Rangers towards the end of the match. But now, the crowd was trying to leave, so they quickly got all their things together and left the stadium.

By now, it was quite dark outside, but Nick decided that they should walk near the football stadium for a while. Evie was so thrilled after the match, she was still talking about it with Nick.

"...and did you see that goal?! It was amazing! How did he get the goal from that distance?! I really didn't think Rangers would win. And then..."

stands	Tribüne
brightly lit	hell erleuchtet
to spread	(sich) ausbreiten
inside	im Inneren

But this time Nick stopped her. They had stopped at a place nearby, at the top of a hill and from here, they could see the entire stadium below, still brightly lit.

Nick looked at her now and spoke very softly, "Evie... I've really liked you for a long time. You're not like all the other girls. I can talk to you about football, you're sporty and I had a really good time with you tonight... I do want to get to know you better. Since it was kind of our first date and my last chance to make it right... I really wanted it to be special for you..."

Evie couldn't believe what she was hearing. She looked into Nick's dark green eyes and a smile was beginning to spread across her face. Nick was standing very close to her and he looked into her eyes, too. Then he bent down, put his arm around her waist and kissed her on the neck.

A wonderful feeling was beginning to spread inside Evie and she could smell his aftershave again. Nick looked at her for a while now, smiling. Then he leaned forward and, this time, he kissed her on the lips. They kissed for what seemed like a very long time while Nick held her very close to him. With his strong grip, he held her around the waist and his cheek gently brushed away her eye make-up. She didn't know how long they had been kissing, but what Evie did know was that sometimes it's best to just be yourself.

Evie and Nick were standing there, both in their jeans and football shirt, but somehow, this really was the perfect first date!

Übung 30: The perfect date. Welcher Dating-Typ bist du? Kreuze jeweils die Beschreibung an, die am besten zu dir passt!

1. Before dating your crush for the first time you feel...
   a) ❑ relaxed, happy, confident.
   b) ❑ unsure, nervous, excited.
   c) ❑ embarrassed, ill, weak

2. At the first date with your favourite boy you wear...
   a) ❑ fancy clothes which make you feel sexy and comfortable.
   b) ❑ the new sexy clothes your best friend convinced you to buy.
   c) ❑ your everyday jeans and jumper.

3. Your favourite boy asks you out. What do you say?
   a) ❑ Great!
   b) ❑ Great! Can I bring my best friend, too?
   c) ❑ Thanks but... are you sure?

4. You have to choose where to go on the first date with your crush. What's your suggestion?
   a) ❑ There's this hip new bar in town. Wanna try it?
   b) ❑ Perhaps we could go to the cinema.
   c) ❑ Oh, I don't know. What do you think?

5. What would *you* do in Evies's position?
   a) ❑ Ignore the blonde girl and ask Nick out on a date.
   b) ❑ Ask my best friend to find out who that blonde girl is.
   c) ❑ Give up thinking of Nick as a boyfriend and just go on daydreaming of him.

Lösungen & Glossar

Lösungen

ÜBUNG 1:

Evie is... ready to go, painted, leaving without saying goodbye, in love with someone.

ÜBUNG 2:

1. turned 2. glanced 3. startled 4. casually 5. crush 6. incredibly

ÜBUNG 3:

1. invitation 2. party 3. surprise 4. birthday 5. outfit 6. Bollywood 7. idea 8. secret

ÜBUNG 4:

1. before – after 2. ask – answer 3. older – younger 4. without – with 5. annoyed – pleased 6. a few – a lot

ÜBUNG 5:

1. Geheimnis 2. in letzter Zeit 3. plötzlich 4. hartnäckig 5. rot werden 6. ein breites Grinsen

ÜBUNG 6:

Mostly a): Just friends – you might think you have a crush, but he could just be your best friend! Does he have feelings for you? If he does, then maybe you should speak to him and see if he thinks this is also just a very good friendship.

Mostly b): Slight crush – you are attracted to his personality and physical appearance. Give yourself time to see if this feeling goes away after a while. It might just be a small crush.

Mostly c): Serious Crush – you have a serious crush on someone! You know a lot about him and you act strangely in front of him. Be more confident and find time to speak to him. This is more than just a crush!

ÜBUNG 7:

1. quick – quickly 2. clear – clearly 3. near – nearly
4. surprised – surprisingly 5. beautiful – beautifully
6. patient – patiently 7. final – finally 8. exotic – exoticly
9. happy – happily

ÜBUNG 8:

1. The boys were more casually dressed.
2. Everyone seemed to be enjoying the party.
3. "I don't know why everyone came so late."
4. The girl was wearing a beautiful Indian dress.
5. Everybody in the whole house began to cheer and sing.
6. Suddenly Evie felt a little jealous.
7. Evie found it strange that she liked Nick so much.
8. Every time she saw him she had butterflies in her stomach.

ÜBUNG 9:

1. guy 2. final 3. wants 4. upset 5. friends 6. blonde

Evie feels unsure.

ÜBUNG 10:

1. with 2. on 3. after 4. through 5. over, to 6. about

ÜBUNG 11:

1. feel – felt 2. meet – met 3. come – came
4. brake – broke 5. give – gave 6. get – got
7. speak – spoke 8. sit – sat

ÜBUNG 12:

Horizontal: birthday, flirting, boyfriend, scarf

Vertikal: princess, blonde

Diagonal: kitchen, turban

E	I	D	P	K	O	N	A	I	C	X	A
N	U	Z	R	B	I	R	T	H	D	A	Y
T	R	F	L	I	R	T	I	N	G	R	P
I	P	F	A	G	H	B	C	A	P	O	A
R	R	S	I	F	T	C	P	H	L	Y	R
E	I	V	Y	A	N	U	W	O	E	Q	E
B	N	M	B	O	Y	F	R	I	E	N	D
C	C	I	L	R	Z	H	N	B	P	L	G
A	E	R	O	E	H	G	A	L	A	W	F
F	S	A	N	K	L	X	B	O	Z	N	I
H	S	E	D	S	C	A	R	F	H	J	L
K	A	T	E	M	A	R	Z	O	G	A	K

ÜBUNG 13:

1. Erfolg – success 2. erfreut – delighted 3. Geständnis – confession 4. Entscheidung – decision 5. Klassenkamerad – classmate 6. Einladung – invitation 7. Kirmes – fair 8. Mut – courage

ÜBUNG 14:

1. bench 2. Saturday 3. camera 4. brother 5. Shakespeare 6. mood 7. Bollywood

ÜBUNG 15:

1. Nina hadn't spoken to any of them.
2. Nina was right.
3. Nina has spoken the truth.
4. The girl could be Nick's girlfriend.
5. No-one had seen her before.
6. Nobody knows the girl's name.

ÜBUNG 16:

1. football 2. disappointed 3. smiling 4. odd 5. classmate 6. sit 7. head 8. set off

ÜBUNG 17:

1. I can't 2. I'm 3. you didn't 4. you're 5. we'll 6. you don't 7. let's 8. they're

ÜBUNG 18:

1. muddy 2. embarrassed 3. surprised 4. strong 5. great 6. jealous 7. biggest 8. tall

ÜBUNG 19:

1. You have been in contact with Nick all the time.
2. You always get attention from boys.
3. You and Nick are friends.
4. You didn't want me to contact him.
5. You fancy Nick yourself!
6. You didn't tell me you had Nick's number!
7. You kept it a secret that you are friends.

ÜBUNG 20:

1	2	3	4	5	6	7
b	*e*	*d*	*c*	*g*	*a*	*f*

ÜBUNG 21:

1. buy candyfloss 2. read her mind 3. wore make-up 4. put on earrings 5. play football 6. walk away 7. enter the fairground 8. queue for a ride

ÜBUNG 22:

1. dodgems 2. candyfloss 3. fairground 4. teenagers 5. music 6. lights 7. amazing

ÜBUNG 23:

1	2	3	4	5	6	7
d	*g*	*b*	*e*	*c*	*a*	*f*

ÜBUNG 24:

1. teddy bear 2. phone 3. candyfloss 4. girl 5. event 6. mood 7. teacups Lösung: dodgems

ÜBUNG 25:

1. quite sad 2. happy 3. enjoys 4. doesnt't know 5. not really want

ÜBUNG 26:

1. crush 2. love 3. jealous 4. Louise 5. practice 6. night
Louise is Nick's cousin!

ÜBUNG 27:

1. laugh – cry 2. sporty – unathletic 3. more – less 4. scared – courageous 5. thrilled – frustrated 6. alone – together 7. hate – love 8. final – first

ÜBUNG 28:

1. thought 2. crush 3. eyelashes 4. uneasy 5. friend 6. doubt

ÜBUNG 29:

1. trainers – Turnschuhe 2. sporty – sportlich 3. stadium – Stadion 4. entrance – Eingang 5. match – Spiel 6. referee – Schiedsrichter 7. team – Mannschaft 8. score – Spielstand 9. half-time – Halbzeit 10. even – unentschieden

ÜBUNG 30:

Mostly a): Lucky girl! You feel confident and you know exactly what you want. At your first date you are really relaxed. But be careful: don't act too cool. This could irritate your favourite boy and make him feel uneasy.

Mostly b): You are attractive and smart. So you don't need to depend on the opinion of others – just be yourself! Remember: it's you your favourite boy is interested in, not your best friend. And more self-esteem will make you even more attractive.

Mostly c): You're romantic and shy. You like to daydream about your favourite boy, but if he asks you out, you get really nervous. Your crush could misunderstand your behaviour and think you aren't really interested in him. So at your first date put on some clothes that make you feel pretty, be positive and show him you really like him.

Glossar

actually	eigentlich
advice	Ratschlag
algebraic expression	algebraische Gleichung
all of a sudden	plötzlich, mit einem Mal
amazed	verwundert
amazingly	überraschend, erstaunlich
annoyed	verärgert
to apply	auftragen, auflegen
to appreciate sth.	dankbar sein (für etw.)
to approach	sich nähern, herankommen
at the sound of	beim Hören von
attacker	Angreifer(in)
to avoid	vermeiden
barely	kaum, fast
to be able to do sth.	etw. tun können
to beam with joy	vor Freude strahlen
to be aware	merken, sich bewusst sein
to be disappointed in sb.	von jmd. enttäuscht sein
behaviour	Benehmen, Verhalten
to be honest	um ehrlich zu sein
to be in the mood	in Stimmung sein
belongings	Siebensachen
bench	Bank
to bend (bent, bent) down	niederknien
to be positive	ganz sicher sein
to be running late	sich verspäten
to be scared	Angst haben
to be tempted	in Versuchung geraten
to be thrilled	sich wahnsinnig freuen

bindi	Bindi, (Schmuck-)Punkt auf der Stirn
to blush	erröten
border	Saum
to borrow	ausleihen
bothered	beunruhigt
to break the silence	das Schweigen brechen
bright	leuchtend
brightly lit	hell erleuchtet
broad-shouldered	breitschultrig
to build up one's courage	seinen Mut sammeln
bumpy	holperig
to burst into laughter	in Gelächter ausbrechen
by the looks of things	*hier:* so wie es aussah
to calm sb.	jmd. beruhigen
candyfloss stand	Zuckerwattestand
candyfloss	Zuckerwatte
casually	lässig
to catch up with sb.	jmd. aufholen
changing room	Umkleidekabine
to chat	quatschen
to cheer	jubeln, klatschen
Cheer up!	Kopf hoch!
to cheer up	aufheitern, bessere Laune bekommen
cheerfully	fröhlich
clearly	deutlich
close	eng befreundet, nah
to come undone	aufgehen
concerned	besorgt
confession	Geständnis
to confront sb.	jmd. zur Rede stellen
confused	verwirrt
to convince	überzeugen
ϟ 'cos	Kurzform von „because"

crowd	*hier:* Clique
crowded	überfüllt
crush	Schwarm
to cry out	aufschreien, ausrufen
curious	neugierig
decision	Entscheidung
to delete	löschen
delighted	hocherfreut
determined	entschlossen
to disagree	anderer Meinung sein
disappointment	Enttäuschung
dishevelled	unordentlich
dissatisfied	unzufrieden
distracted	unaufmerksam, abgelenkt
dodgems	Autoscooter
done	fertig
to doubt sb.	jmd. misstrauen
draw	Unentschieden
to dress up	sich verkleiden, sich schick machen
to drift apart	auseinander gehen
ecstatic	total begeistert
either of them	eine(r) von beiden
embarrassment	Verlegenheit
embarrassing	peinlich
enthusiasm	Begeisterung
entire	ganz, gesamt
entrance	Eingang
equally	genauso, gleichermaßen
even	*hier:* unentschieden
eventful	erlebnisreich
eventually	schließlich, letztendlich
excitement	Begeisterung
to exclaim	rufen, ausrufen
excuse	Ausrede

exhausted	erschöpft
eyelashes	Wimpern
fair	Kirmes
fairground ride	Karussell
fairground	Festplatz
fairly	ziemlich
to fall (fell, fallen) off	runterfallen
ϟ to fancy sb.	jmd. toll finden
fancy	schick
fancy-dress party	Mottoparty
final	Finale
to finish (off)	erledigen
firm grip	fester Griff
ϟ fit	attraktiv
fool	Dummkopf, Narr
foolish	dumm
forehead	Stirn
ϟ funky	abgefahren
furious	wütend
ϟ fuss	Aufregung
fussy	wählerisch, aufgeregt
game tactic	taktischer Spielzug
ϟ Get a move on!	Los, mach schon!
to get attention from sb.	jmd. auffallen, von jmd. beachtet werden
to get in the way	in die Quere kommen
ϟ Get this!	Hör dir das an!
to giggle	kichern
to glance	blicken
to go after sb.	jmd. nachlaufen
good-looking	gut aussehend
to grab	greifen
grateful	dankbar
grip	Griff
to grumble	grummeln, murren

to guess about sth.	etw. erraten
to guess	raten
ϟ Guys!	Leute!
half-time	Halbzeit
to hand in	einreichen, abgeben
to hang around with sb.	mit jmd. herumhängen
Hang on a second!	Warte eine Sekunde!
harsh	barsch
hastily	hastig
ϟ to have a crush on sb.	in jmd. verknallt sein
to have butterflies in one's stomach	Schmetterlinge im Bauch haben
to have sth. in mind	etw. im Sinn haben
to have the courage to do sth.	den Mut haben, etw. zu tun
to head towards	zusteuern auf
hilarious	urkomisch
hip	Hüfte
to hug	umarmen
hug	Umarmung
in pretty good shape	ziemlich gut in Form
incredibly	unglaublich
inside	im Inneren
insistent	hartnäckig
to introduce sb.	jmd. vorstellen
invitation	Einladung
ϟ invite	Einladung
jealous	eifersüchtig
to jog off	loslaufen
to join sb.	zu jmd. hingehen
Keep it up!	Mach weiter so!
to kid	scherzen
ϟ kinda (kind of)	irgendwie
lace	Schnürsenkel
to lead (led, led) sb. away	jmd. wegführen
to lean (lent, lent) against	lehnen an/gegen

to let go of sth.	etw. loslassen
to look stunning	umwerfend aussehen
lunchtime	Mittagszeit
to manage to do sth.	schaffen, etw. zu tun
massive crowd	große Menschenmenge
ϟ mate	Kumpel, Freund
mean	gemein, böse
mess	Chaos, Durcheinander
mock exam	Probeprüfung
modest	bescheiden
muddy	schmutzig, veschlammt
mug	Becher, große Tasse
to mumble	murmeln, brummeln
murmur	Murmeln
necklace	Halskette
neither..., nor	weder ..., noch
neither of them	keine(r) von ihnen
to nod (in agreement)	(zustimmend) nicken
none of them	keine(r) von ihnen
ϟ not that much of a big deal	keine so große Sache
obviously	offensichtlich
odd	merkwürdig
otherwise	ansonsten
to overhear (overheard, overheard)	hören
to overreact	überreagieren
packed lunch	Lunchpaket
packed	überfüllt
to panic	panisch werden
particularly	besonders
to pat sb. on the back	jmd. auf die Schulter klopfen
pat	Klaps
pathetic	jämmerlich, erbärmlich
patiently	geduldig
pearl	Perle

performance	Leistung
to pick up	aufheben, mitnehmen
to pick up the phone	den Hörer abnehmen
playfully	spielerisch
pleasantly surprised	angenehm überrascht
pleased	erfreut, zufrieden
to predict	voraussagen
to prefer	bevorzugen
to queue up	Schlange stehen
queue	Schlange
to realize	feststellen, bemerken
to reassure sb.	jmd. beruhigen
to recognize	(an)erkennen
referee	Schiedsrichter
relieved	erleichtert
to remain silent	schweigen, nichts sagen
remarkably	bemerkenswert
ridiculous	lächerlich
right on time	zur rechten Zeit
to roll one's eyes	mit den Augen rollen
romantic	Romantiker(in)
round-faced	pausbäckig
rude	unhöflich, ruppig
rumour	Gerücht
to rush off	(davon)eilen
safe	sicher, gefahrlos
scarf	Halstuch
to score a goal	ein Tor schießen
score	Spielstand
ϟ to scream and shout	herumtoben
secretly	heimlich, insgeheim
to seem	erscheinen
to see the bigger picture	das Ganze sehen
to set exercises	Übungen aufgeben
to set (set, set) off	sich auf den Weg machen

shawl	Schal
to shriek out	hinausschreien
to shrug one's shoulders	mit den Schultern zucken
to shudder	zittern
shy	schüchtern
siblings	Geschwister
silk	Seide
skip of joy	Freudensprung
to slam	zuschlagen
sleeping bag	Schlafsack
something she could not argue with	etwas, wogegen sie nichts sagen konnte
to sort sth. out	etw. klären, planen
to spin (span, spun) round	herumwirbeln
splendid	fantastisch
sporty	sportlich
to spot	sehen, entdecken
to spread (spread, spread)	(sich) ausbreiten
to squeal	(auf)jubeln
to squeeze	drücken
stadium	Stadion
stall	Verkaufsstand
to stammer	stammeln, stottern
to stand (stood, stood) up	aufstehen
stands	Tribüne
to startle from	aufschrecken aus
to state	angeben, festsetzen
to stay behind	(zurück)bleiben
to step off	aussteigen
striker	Stürmer
to suggest	vorschlagen
to support	befürworten, unterstützen
to suppose	vermuten
surprise	Überraschung
sweatband	Schweißband

sweaty	verschwitzt
sweet	süß, lieb
sympathetic	mitfühlend
to talk in whispers	im Flüsterton sprechen
to tap on sb.'s shoulder	jmd. auf die Schulter klopfen
teacups	Teetassen (-Karussell)
tear	Träne
tearful	weinerlich
Tell me about it!	Wem sagst du das!
tense	angespannt, nervös
textbook	Lehrbuch
that was really lucky!	das war wirklich ein Glück!
thicket of bushes	Gebüsch
to Evie's (house)	bei/zu Evie
toffee apples	kandierte Äpfel
towards	nach, in Richtung
tracksuit bottoms	Trainingshose
trainers	Turnschuhe
to turn away	sich abwenden
to turn back	umkehren
unaware	nichts ahnend, unwissend
uneasy	unbehaglich
unexpected	unerwartet
unless	es sei denn, dass
upcoming	anstehend
to upset (upset, upset)	verärgern
waist	Taille
waistcoat	Weste
to wait one's turn	warten, bis man an der Reihe ist
Was it just Evie?	Kam es Evie nur so vor?
to waste time	Zeit verschwenden
to wave	winken
to wave sb. goodbye	jmd. zum Abschied winken
weakly	schwach

weird	seltsam
ϟ We'll catch up with you some other time!	Wir sehen uns demnächst!
what's more	darüber hinaus, außerdem
ϟ Whatever is the matter?	Was ist denn los?
ϟ whereabouts	wo etwa
whether	ob
to whisper	flüstern
whistle	Trillerpfeife
to wink at sb.	jmd. zuzwinkern
to wonder	sich überlegen
worth the effort	die Mühe wert
to wrap	einschlagen, (um)wickeln
wrist	Handgelenk
to yell at sb.	jmd. anschreien
ϟ yep	ja; jo (ugs.)
ϟ you lot	ihr da